Jamal Qaiser
Sadaf Taimur

Simmering Kashmir

Jamal Qaiser
Sadaf Taimur

Simmering Kashmir

Diplomatic Council Publishing

1st edition 2020

© 2020 Diplomatic Council Publishing, Mühlhohle 2, 65205 Wiesbaden, Germany

Bibliographic information from the German National Library

The German National Library lists this publication in the German National Bibliography; Detailed bibliographic data are available on the Internet at http://dnb.d-nb.de.Printed in the Federal Republic of Germany.

Cover design: Tanveer Ahmed Khan

Printed on acid-free paper.

Print ISBN: 978-3-947818-11-2

E-Book: 978-3-947818-12-9

About the Authors

Jamal Qaiser

The German-Pakistani entrepreneur, writer, Peace Activist and Social Potential Advisor Jamal Qaiser, is an OPM Graduate of the prestigious Harvard Business School, Post-Graduate of The Globe Business College Munich and has completed a course in "Transition to Leadership" from Oxford University.

Jamal Qaiser advises various companies and political parties, NGOs, humanist organizations and governmental apparatus. Since 2016 he has advised as UN-Commissioner for UN-Affairs for the Diplomatic Council the economic and UN Social Council - one think tank at the United Nations has the highest consultative status, i.e. the Economic and Social Council of the UN. His book published in 2016: "Der fremde Erfolgsfaktor – Why we urgently need immigrants in Germany", attracted a great deal of attention both nationally and internationally. In the same year he won the international getAbstract Book Award with his work from a selection of over 10,000 non-fiction books. Jamal Qaiser also supports Ubiquity University in transformative education for social impact as Special Liaison to the United Nations.

As a published academic and renowned business and social-political consultant, Mr. Qaiser's contributions to global organizations such as the United Nations, The WTO, The German

Federal Ministry of Commerce and ASEAN have been significant. He has also worked tirelessly as an entrepreneur and an innovator, driving multi-million-dollar business ventures as the CEO of Qaiser Equity Investments. Perhaps most telling are his life-changing contributions to humanitarian and philanthropic efforts in Pakistan and around the world through the charity "Humanity First."

Sadaf Taimur

Sadaf is a Doctoral Scholar at University of Tokyo and Japan Society for the Promotion of Science (JSPS) Fellow. She has 6 years of experience in education and development sector, during which she has: (a) Worked as member of Silver Oaks Schools & College System; (b) Managed Communications, Advocacy & Youth Mobilization at Idara-e-Taleem-o-Aagahi (ITA)-Center of Education & Consciousness; (c) Worked as Executive Director at Youth General Assembly (a social movement, to train & mobilize youth to work on UN's Sustainable Development Agenda, which she co-founded) & (d) Worked as an Advisory Mentor for Queen's Young Leaders Program (UK).

As G20 Global Changer, she was involved in proposing recommendations, on education for sustainable development, for G20 leaders which were presented at G20 Summit, 2017 (Germany). Sadaf sits on Advisory Board of "Global Education Conference", U.S.A. and serve as an SDG expert at Digital Human Library (dHL), Canada.

She is also involved in the Education for Global Peace Project under University of California Irvine (UCI), as a researcher, on peace education. Sadaf won GESS (Global Education Supplies & Solutions) Outstanding Contribution in Education for Sustainable Development Award, 2016 (Dubai). She got selected as Dalai Lama Fellow (U.S.A) to implement "compassion in action project". She represented Pakistan: as Youth Delegate UNESCO-MGIEP at "UNESCO week for peace & sustainable development: role of education" (Canada) and as Youth Champion at Rise Up's Youth Champions Initiative Incubator (U.S.A.).

Contents

Preamble

Kashmir is a long-standing conflict between India and Pakistan and we are aware that resolving it or even talking about this is a daunting task. But this is certainly not impossible!

Jamal Qaiser (author), as Diplomatic Council' Commissioner for UNO Affairs, gave a statement on Kashmir at the United Nations, last year and talked about potential threats related to Kashmir conflict and proposed solutions as well. Just after his speech, he met the Indian delegation at the United Nations and discussed the economic repercussions of Kashmir conflict. While talking to the delegation, Jamal Qaiser highlighted that for countries to flourish economically resolving Kashmir issue is crucial and urgent. Indian delegation agreed to what he was saying but mentioned that we can only agree to this off the record as we have a policy and we have to comply to that. The delegation appreciated how Jamal Qaiser presented the solution to the long-standing Kashmir issue. At this point he decided to write a book on this issue.

We understand that region cannot achieve stability economically or socially until the Kashmir conflict is resolved but on the other hand many Kashmiris are also deprived of their basic rights. In the modern civilized world, now, the Kashmir issue should not be about how much land a country is going to get but it should be about justice and prosperity in the region.

This book talks about the history of sub-continent starting from 16th century and discusses the British invasion, partition of the sub-continent and political games after the partition as well. The book tried to throw some light on the connection between the British invasion and Hindu-Muslim segregation followed by hatred, partition of the region, Kashmir conflict and lack of trust between two states. We also tried to underlie what went wrong on both sides and what can be done to.

Sadaf Taimur (author), being a researcher and member of Education for Global Peace, University of California-Irvine, is a strong advocate of peacebuilding and emphasize on how peace is connected to all other sustainability challenges. In February 2019, when she planned her visit to Pakistan with an accompanying Japanese colleague, her colleague got really anxious regarding visiting Pakistan because of the on-going Pakistan-India conflict. She even showed some hesitation and fear as the international media was reporting the fear of nuclear war in the region. Sadaf Taimur had to deliver a workshop to young people (as a Chair at Youth General Assembly) regarding education for peacebuilding. Because of the ongoing circumstances she incorporated the Kashmir resolution segment in her workshop. This segment was highly appreciated by the young people participating in the workshop and all of them gave very positive responses regarding its resolution. At that time, she felt that there is a need to talk about Kashmir resolution and engage more people. During the same visit, Sadaf Taimur met Jamal Qaiser for some official purpose and at that point this book was formally conceptualized.

This book presents the point of views, first and foremost as DC Commissioner for UN Affairs, in the attempt to portray this complex situation as a neutral observer. One of the authors, Jamal Qaiser, has been representing the Diplomatic Council as UN-Commissioner for UN-Affairs since 2016. The Diplomatic

Council is a global think tank that sees itself as a bridge between diplomacy, on the one hand, and business and society on the other. It is a UN-accredited organization with special consultative status with the Economic and Social Council of the United Nations.

Jamal Qaiser's statement regarding Kashmir at the United Nations and the following conversation with the Indian delegation led to this book, and we have written it for those readers who seek a peaceful solution to the Kashmir conflict, who crave world peace, who have the foresight not to be influenced by war propaganda in politics and the media.

In spite of the difficult situation, we trust that this conflict will be resolved peacefully and that our next generations will also live in peace. For us to succeed, we must all make our contribution. No-one can evade this responsibility.

Yours

Jamal Qaiser & Sadaf Taimur

Chapter 1 – The British Rule in the Sub-Continent

After Spanish Armada's defeat, in 1588, the merchants of London presented a petition to the Queen Elizabeth 1: asking her permission to sail to the Indian Ocean. In 1591, on The Queen's permission, three ships sailed from Torbay to the Arabian Sea. This was one of the earliest, English, overseas Indian missions. Three more ships sailed towards Arabian Sea in the year 1596 but all of them were lost in the sea and never reached their destination. Another group of merchants, with an intention to sail to the East Indies, applied for the Queen's support in 1599. Failed in the initial attempt, the group tried again a year later and succeeded. These merchants were eventually known as 'Adventurers'.

An Unfair Charter

After their success in 1600, a Royal Charted to "George, Earl of Cumberland, and 215 Knights, Aldermen, and Burgesses" was granted by the Queen under the name 'Governor and Company of Merchants' of London trading with the East Indies. In the light of this charter, the newly formed company exercised monopoly for 15 years with all the countries of the west of the Straits of Magellan and the Cape of Good Hope. All the people who wanted to trade were supposed to obtain a license from a company and anyone who traded in a way to breach the charter was liable of penalty on their cargo and ships (half of which went to the company and a half to the royal palace); along with imprisonment at the "royal pleasure".

Clearly, the charter was not fair, as it was intentionally created to serve the royal palace and create disparities in the region.

During the years 1601 and 1608, four expeditions took Britain to East Indies in order to establish trade. The company, also known as East India Company (EIC), struggled with the trade of spice because they had to compete with well-established Dutch Company. On the first voyage, EIC opened a factory in Bantam. For 20 years pepper imports from Java remained an important part of company's trade. Afterwards, EIC established its first company in Bengal, South India. Upon landing in India, EIC reported high profits which convinced King James I to grant subsidiary licenses to other trading companies in England. King James I renewed the charter given to EIC for an indefinite period. However, a clause was included in the charter stating that the charter would cease if there is no profit from trade for three consecutive years. Several conflicts occurred between the English traders and their Portuguese and Dutch counterparts in the Indian Ocean.

EIC decided to exploit the opportunity and get a foothold in mainland India with official permission of Mughal Empire and Britain. For this purpose, they requested the

Crown to launch a diplomatic mission to India. Instructed by King James 1, in 1612, Sir Thomas Roe visited the Mughal Emperor Nuruddin Salim Jahangir to arrange for a commercial treaty. This treaty was to provide the company with the rights to establish factories and reside in Surat and other areas. EIC, in return, promised to provide Mughal Emperor with the rarities and goods from European market. This mission was remarkably successful, as the greed for goods and material was not one-sided.

From a Company to an Administrative Body

On being provided with imperial support, the company expanded its operations regarding commercial trade and took the lead over the Portuguese company which had bases in Bombay, Goa and Chittagong. These bases were ceded to England by Portugal. By 1647, EIC ended up having 90 employees and 23 factories in India. The Portuguese and Spanish influence in the region reduced, leaving intense competition between Dutch East India Company and EIC. This extreme competition led to Anglo-Dutch Wars in the 17th and 18th centuries.

With an aim to strengthen the power of the EIC, King Charles II granted EIC the permission to autonomously acquire command forts, territory, money, and troop and to form alliances. EIC was also allowed to make peace and war and to exercise criminal and civil jurisdictions over the acquired territories. So, the intentions of trade converted into the intentions to rule; and EIC was converted from a trading company to a *de facto* administrative agent demonstrating strong powers granted by the British government.

The affluence of the EIC officers not only allowed them to return to Britain but obtain political power by establishing businesses and properties. Later, EIC developed a lobby in the English parliament under the pressure from the company associates and tradesmen who wanted to establish private companies in India. This led to a deregulating act that was passed in 1694. This act terminated the charter, which was in order for around 100 years, and allowed English firms to trade with India (unless specifically prohibited by the parliament). Another act was passed in 1698 which allowed the establishment of another "parallel" East India Company (officially known as English Company Trading to East Indies). The two companies wrestled with each other for an overriding share in trade, both in India and England. After some time, it became clear that it was difficult to compete with the original company. Hence, in 1708, the two companies merged and became: The *United Company of Merchants of England trading to the East Indies.*

The advent of the industrial revolution put Britain far ahead of its rivals in Europe. The level of production, demand, growth, and success made Britain popular in overseas trade. EIC's private army was prepared to facilitate the company with skills required to assert its interests in the new regions of India without any hindrance from other colonial powers. However, local rulers continuously showed resistance towards EIC.

On the other hand, in 1755, Siraj ud Daulah became Nawab of Bengal adopting a pro-French policy in India. He invaded the British trading posts, including Calcutta. Lieutenant Colonel Robert Clive was sent from Madras to retake Calcutta and afterward they started plotting the defeat of Nawab. British secretly bribed some of the Bengali generals and Mir Jafar (one of the discontented followers of Nawab). Clive, then, started to advance towards Bengal's capital and was confronted by Nawab's army at Plassey (Palashi) by Bhaghirathi River. Seeing Nawab's army, which was backed with French artillerymen, it was very difficult to foresee British victory. Nawab lost the battle because of the deception from his people. In 1757, during the Battle of Plassey, EIC defeated the ruler of Bengal and his French allies and re-established the company's presence in Bengal. From that day onward, with each passing day, EIC started to function more like an administrative body and less as a trading company.

The Indian Rebellion Leading to British Raj

With the help of EIC's private army, the company was able to assert its interests in the new regions of India without any hindrance from other colonial powers. However, local rulers continuously showed resistance towards EIC. The powers of EIC proliferated in the sub-continent and took two forms. The first form was taking control of Indian states and then governing the underlying regions. The second form was signing treaties with the local rulers to accept EIC's authority in the region in return of limited internal autonomy.

The EIC's independent armies expanded to a total of 280,000 men as they started recruiting local people in their army. Their Bengal Army ended up including land-owning Muslims and high-caste Hindus. In EIC's army, British officers were always placed on top of local Indians; irrespective of their service and experience. The local officers were not allowed to take part in any leadership or administrative training, so as to make sure that they stay dependent on the British Officers. This strategy, over time, gained dissatisfaction among the local Indian soldiers. Some grievances of the local soldiers were developed against EIC administration because of the ethnic gaps that existed between the British officers and their local Indian troops. In 1857, the British officers asked the local soldiers to use the newly introduced gunpowder cartridges. These cartridges were made from pig and cow fat and loading these cartridges required them to tear it with their teeth. This was taken as an insult to the religious practices of Hindus and Muslims. This act of lack of ethnic sensitivity on part of British officers and EIC administration converted the dissatisfaction of the local soldiers into revolt and aggression. This served as the major trigger of the Indian Rebellion of 1857. The rebellion of Indian soldiers was exacerbated by local peasant and community armies who joined the Indian soldiers in the rebellion against EIC. Community armies were formed because of the underlying objections on British taxation and land captures. This was the time when Hindus and Muslims, irrespective of their faiths, were fighting against slavery, injustice, and disrespect. They revolted against the ethnic insensitivity of Britishers because they were aware that ethnic identities should be respected. This also reflects that Hindus and Muslims were living in harmony and they were used to respecting each other's religions. If they were not respecting each other, they wouldn't have expected the same from the Britishers and they wouldn't have revolted.

As a result of the Indian rebellion of 1858, EIC was dissolved and got nationalized by the British government. British restructured the financial system, the army and the administration in India. The crown started governing the country directly and the British Raj, as a colonial rule, was FORMALLY established in the Indian Sub-continent. The British Raj remained in the subcontinent through the years 1858-1947.

The British Raj was extended all over the present-day: Pakistan, India and Bangladesh (excluding some areas which were then held by other European nations e.g. Goa and Pondicherry). The sub-continent area is known for its diversity with fertile floodplains, Himalayan mountain ranges, a long coastline, Indo-Gangetic plain, arid uplands, tropical dry forests, and the Thar Desert.

The Civilizing Mission

The "civilizing mission" was used as a rationale to justify the imperial control of the subcontinent. This mission aimed at introducing limited reforms to produce a qualified, white-collar, workforce which could loyally support the colonial rule. The same rationale was used by the British to establish colonies in other Asian and African countries. The British not only governed these colonies but they also tried to westernize them by implementing a colonial ideology i.e. "assimilation". The concept of racism emerged with the concept of the "civilizing mission" where British saw the "backward" nation in the subcontinent as incapable of achieving, what British perceived as, an advanced level of social development. Therefore, they decided to "civilize" the sub-continent and colonized it by influencing the indigenous elites in order to get loyal local support for the imperial rule.

The main focus of the "civilizing mission" in the subcontinent was to introduce educational reforms. The perception of the imperial rule was that 'English' will speed up modernization in the region. Hence, the English language became a high priority. Thomas Babington Macaulay was amongst one of the most influential reformers. Macaulay, having a utilitarian approach, believed the Sub-continent had nothing to teach regarding modernization or modern skills and therefore education should happen in English so as to maintain the quality. Macaulay urged the Governor-General to reform the secondary education to deliver "useful learning"; and he equated "useful learning" to Western culture. He argued that Sanskrit and Persian, as languages, do not serve the purpose of "useful learning" and these languages are also less accessible than English. Macaulay did not know either Sanskrit or Persian, but he claimed that Western experts have a consensus that a single shelf of the western library is equal to the whole native literature of Sanskrit and Persian. Hence, he advocated for implementation of the Western English curriculum after the sixth year of schooling. This strategy was designed to create a class of local Indians who could serve as cultural intermediaries between the people of the sub-continent and British. According to Macaulay, creating this class was essential before reforming the overall education system. The "civilization mission" soon became an explanation for racism and British misrule, and this time British did not even pretend that the progress of the sub-continent was ever a goal. The advocators of real reform and prosperity of the region became less influential. This led the British to assume that Indians had to be ruled with an iron hand. Democratic opportunities for the people of the sub-continent were postponed for an indefinite period. Most of the debate on the role of Britain in sub-continent took place in Britain, this allowed the imperialist and the general population at home to believe that "civilizing mission" was working well. The imperial support in Britain got strengthened with the help of this fake campaign: "civilizing mission".

The economy of the British ruled sub-continent was designed in a way to serve the British economy. The British collaborated with local elites to make this strategy successful. These elites also benefited from many British induced economic changes. In the second half of the 19th century and with the advent of the industrial revolution; railway, canals, roads, and bridges were built rapidly, and telegraph links were established. The major purpose of establishing these channels was to export raw materials, most notably cotton, from the sub-continent to England. The finished goods from England were then transported back for sale in Indian markets.

The industrialization in the sub-continent remained limited, although Britain was considered as one of the global leaders of industrial development. Despite colonizing the space, Britain did not accept any ties with the sub-continent. "Civilizing mission" was used, ONLY, as a buzz word to justify colonization. Self-interest of the British rule was the main reason that caused stagnation of industrial and economic development in the British colonized India. Before colonization, in the 17th century, India was a relatively commercialized and urbanized country. India used to export not only textile but silk, spices, and rice and was recognized as one of the main producers of cotton textiles in the world. After colonization, in late the 18th century, the cotton industry went through technological revolution, but Indian industry and economy stayed stagnant. British control over the export of cheap Manchester cotton; and trade, on the whole, are significant reasons to explain why Indian industrialization and economy stagnated. Some of the historians also mentioned that because India was much more agricultural as compared to Britain, therefore the wages in Britain were relatively higher. This allowed cotton producers in Britain to invent and purchase new expensive technologies. An open question arises here: if there was control on the trade and exports how were cotton producers of the sub-continent expected to improve their financial capacity or to increase the wage rate or to buy expensive technology?

The Indian textile export declined significantly through the 19th century, though Indian cotton was recognized universally for its quality. High tariffs imposed on Indian textile factories and British restrictions on Indian cotton imports transformed India into the source of raw cotton rather than the source of textiles.

Backed by private investors, the new railway companies were encouraged by the colonial government to build rail systems in India. The government guaranteed up to a 5% annual return to the private companies in the initial years of operation. The companies started building the railway lines under a 99-year lease with a condition that the government has the discretion to buy them earlier. With the guarantee system, investments started flowing in the subcontinent and new rail companies developed. By the late 19th century, a modern railway system was developed with the help of British engineers and investors. The British government was supportive of this development because they realized the value of railway system for military use in case of another rebellion and the value it can be off for economic growth. As the railway projects were run by private British companies, funding, management, engineers and skilled craftsmen came from Britain. Initially, only unskilled workforce was hired from India (locality). Until the 1930's, only Europeans were hired as managers, engineers and skilled workforce by the British companies. Similarly, the railway system was designed and built to serve the British companies and, indirectly: the British economy. The colonial government wanted the bids on the railway system contracts to happen in London, (to be made in remote Indian office) and this shut down the chances for Indian firms to bid. The spare parts and the hardware for the railway system were purchased from Britain. The railway maintenance workshops in India, run by locals, were not allowed to either manufacture or repair locomotives.

The destruction of India's traditional handicraft industries can be attributed to the spread of railway network. The trains filled with the cheap and mass-manufactured goods, imported from England, reached the inland towns for distribution. This distribution led to the decreased sales of rough, handmade, products from the Indian craftsmen. The handicrafts villages lost their traditional markets and the craftsmen were forced to abandon their creativity and change their livelihoods to agriculture. By the end of the 19th century, three fourth of the sub-continent's population was dependent on agriculture. Hence, there was an increase in the pressure of the population on arable land.

In the years 1880 to 1920, the population and the economy of sub-continent grew at the same rate: 1% per year. On average, there were no long-term changes in income levels. During this period, agriculture remained dominant and extensive agriculture system was built to support the growth of cash crops for exports and as raw material for local industry. The impact of British intervention on sub-continent's economic development still remains a question mark. A British politician, Edmund Burke, in 1780 attacked EIC by mentioning that its top officials had ruined the Indian society and economy. Rajat Kanta Ray, an Indian historian, continued this debate in 1998 and argued that the new economy brought by the British in the 18th century served the British Empire only; it was plunder and a disaster for the traditional economy of the Mughal Empire. Ray also accused the British for imposing high taxes and depleting money and food stocks from the sub-continent, which led to the Bengal famine of 1770 - killing one-third of the population in the city.

According to another British historian, Peter James Marshall, British were not in full control of the sub-continent but were a player in an Indian play and then it rose to power with the help of strong support and collaboration with Indian elites. However, there is a consensus between many historians that British rule did not fix the divisive and hierarchal caste-based system of the Indian society and that is the reason ordinary people from the sub-continent remained excluded from the benefits of economic growth.

Coming back to the "civilizing mission" concept which was used by the British rule to justify colonization, it did not achieve its purpose but instead eroded the culture, society, and economy of the continent in so many ways.

In 1885, Indians and some British members formed The Indian National Congress (INC). The objective of INC was to advocate that there shall be greater share for the educated Indians/locals in the government and to create a platform that promotes political dialogue between British Raj and educated Indians. The first session of this dialogue happened in 1885 with 72 delegates, representing each province of India. After the formation of INC; particularly after its first session, the congress faced opposition from the British government. According to the INC, an independence movement was the only way that would allow the emergence of a new political system in which INC could be a major party. Hence, the congress eventually decided to advocate for the independence movement.

The initial arguments laid by the Congress were about the reduction of "home charges". In their view, the Indian budget that went to the Indian official budget (taken by the Britishers) and pensions of retired officials who were living in Britain. Another argument raised by INC, under the leadership of Dadabhai Naoroji, was the economic drain argument. According to this argument the poverty in India was the result of British exploitation of the sub-continent and annual loot of gold, silver and other raw materials. Amongst the resolutions by INC, call for the reduction in the military budget and re-imposition of import tariffs on British manufactured goods were also included.

The Political Struggles

In 1905, the first partition of Bengal happened that brought the province to the brink of rebellion. At that time the British recognized that with a population of 85 million, Bengal is too large to be a single province. They decided to divide it. The line was drawn by Lord Curzon's government. The line was cut through the heart of Bengali speaking nation and left western Bengal's *bhadralok*, intellectual Hindu leadership of Calcutta, connected to much less politically active Oriya and Bihari speaking Hindus on their south and north. On the eastern end of Bengal, a new Muslim majority province was created with Eastern Bengal and Assam. The congress's leadership viewed this partition as an attempt to "divide and rule";

whereas, the British government tried to suppress the voices of *bhadralok* intellectuals by dividing them. The partition of Bengal was a strategy to strengthen the British rule in the region. The British leadership recognized that if they wouldn't create a divide between Hindus and Muslims, they could face strong rejection and mutiny from the people of India. Mass protests and rallies before and after the partition of Bengal attracted millions of people. As a reaction against the partition, Hindus in Bengal launched a mass boycott of British manufactured goods. Instead of foreign-made clothes, Indians started to put on domestic cotton and other clothing items that were manufactured in the sub-continent. This movement, known as swadeshi movement, led to stimulating domestic enterprises in various fields including Indian cotton mills, glassblowing shops, and iron and steel factories etc.

Congress emerged as an all-India political platform, but it failed to attract Muslims of the sub-continent. The Muslims started to feel that their representation in the government service was inadequate. As a response, in 1906, the All-India Muslim League was founded. Muhammad Ali Jinnah, the leader of the league joined INC, in 1916. Initially, Jinnah did not want independent, outright self-rule. According to his view, British influence on education, law, industry, and culture was beneficial for the subcontinent. In order to secure the interest of Muslim diaspora in the sub-continent, Jinnah had to change his thinking and the league ended up playing a decisive role in

1940's Indian independence movement. However, Jinnah never wanted partition between the sub-continent and was an ambassador of Hindu-Muslim unity. Jinnah joined INC and Muslim League together to ensure cooperation between the two organizations and he firmly believed that cooperation and unity were essential for the establishment of self-government.

In 1915 Mahatma Gandhi came back from South Africa and took the position of president of the congress. He formed an alliance with Khilafat Movement: which was a political Islamic protest campaign launched by Muslims to promote Hindu-Muslim unity and to influence the British government. Khilafat Movement got weakened and collapsed after the World War-I as Muslims working with the congress were divided into the Khilafat Movement and the Muslim League. In 1916, Jinnah achieved success in convincing the two organizations (INC and Muslim League) to present a common set of demands to the British Government in the form of Lucknow Pact. With time, the Congress got strongly affiliated with Gandhi who remained its spiritual leader and icon and Jinnah got marginalized in the Indian politics with his emergence. Jinnah wanted to keep politics away from spiritual practices and he insisted that the Congress should call his rival "Mr. Gandhi" instead of calling him 'Mahatma': which means great soul. With this demand, Jinnah was booed off in the Congress by its members. The mutual dislike kept growing between the two leaders.

During World War-I, Britain declared war against Germany on behalf of India, without taking consent from Indian leaders. More than 1.3 million Indian soldiers served in the British Army and a total of 43,000 Indian soldiers died during the war. Most to the Indians supported the British flag but Punjab and Bengal were not easy to control. As, in those regions, many Indians were eager to get independence and they were working in the leadership of Gandhi.

Initially, some Indians had a feeling that Gandhi's ideas and strategies were impractical because they were based on non-violent civil disobedience and those ideas and strategies had to be implemented non-violently by withdrawing cooperation with the corrupt state. Ultimately, Gandhi's vision brought millions of ordinary Indians together in the movement which was then transformed into a national movement instead of elitist struggle. The INC aimed at eradicating poverty, caste differences, and religious and ethnic divisions and because of these aims Congress became a strong group dominating the independence movement in the sub-continent. The members of INC were mostly Hindus, but it had some members from other religions and different economic classes. In 1929, under the presidency of Jawaharlal Nehru, the INC declared that complete independence is their goal. In 1936-37 the British government decided to allow provincial elections in eleven provinces of the sub-continent. As a result of these elections, INC gained power in eight provinces. According to Jinnah, Muslims got betrayed in 1937 elections and their concerns were not addressed adequately. As a consequence, he started advocating for divorce from the Congress out of his fear that even independent India's political life will be dominated by Hindus and will not cater to other minorities. Furthermore, Muslims had to play a pivotal role in the political life of independent India and that is the reason they also deserved the right to have a role in the decision made regarding independence. Jinnah, at that time also emphasized that Hindus and Muslims were two different nations, and both deserved the right to have a representation in politics as their needs were different.

In 1939, the British Viceroy declared that India would enter the World War-II and he did not consult the provincial government while making this announcement. In retaliation, INC asked all the elected representatives to resign from the government and this movement became well known as "Quit India Movement". British government started to lose support as INC was becoming strong at that time. British government resented it strongly. As a result of this movement, Gandhi and Nehru were arrested by the British rule. Around 30,000 Indian soldiers, who were the war prisoners, were recruited by Germans and Japanese to fight against Allies for freedom. While INC and its leaders were involved in the "Quit India Movement", Jinnah remained loyal to the British government and earned their sympathies. After the war was over, the INC leaders were released. Gandhi started calling Jinnah an "evil genius" and a "maniac" and Nehru thought that "he is an example of lack of civilized mind".

Chapter II – Hindu-Muslim-Conflict

British imperial rule in the sub-continent identified that heightened contrasts between Hindus and Muslims would be beneficial for the British rule. There were some deliberate attempts to rewrite Indian history and to portray Muslims as prosecutors and oppressors of Hindus. This was done to receive appreciation from the Hindus of the sub-continent which was the bulk of the population. On the other hand, British rule tried making Muslims aware of "what could happen if Hindus would come in power as a majority" and this created a wave of fear among Muslims of the sub-continent and they became fearful of revenge from Hindus. In this way, British rule succeeded in creating a division among Hindus and Muslims. On one hand, British rule was busy implementing the 'divide and rule' strategy. On the other hand, Hindu majority party i.e. INC did not actively consider the inclusion of the Muslims in the party. Both of these factors gradually created a strong division between Hindus and Muslims.

Division between Hindus and Muslims

As India moved towards its independence, the Muslims started separating themselves from the Hindu majority organizations and established their own Muslim dominant organization i.e. Muslim League. There were two dominant political organizations (Muslim League and INC) in the sub-continent and both of these organizations fought not only against the British rule but also against each other. The continuous clashes between the Muslim League and INC on important issues weakened the strength of Indian people in the British parliament. However, with these conflicts, it was very clear that all the Indian people were demanding self-rule in the sub-continent. The pressure from the league and INC kept increasing on the British rule. Ultimately, after the Second World War when Britain was drained economically and could not maintain the rule over the sub-continent, the Britain decided to leave the sub-continent. Congress and League voted for partition of the sub-continent into two separate countries, i.e. India and Pakistan; based on religion. There is no doubt that at the time of partition both parties agreed that Hindus and Muslims were two different nations and could not co-exist. However, this ideology was built overtime during British rule due to their intervention in the continent.

According to the founder of Pakistan: Muhammad Ali Jinnah: *"Hindus and Muslims belong to two different religious philosophies, social customs and literary traditions. They neither intermarry nor eat together, and indeed they belong to two different civilizations which are based mainly on conflicting ideas and conceptions"*.

The Exit of Britain

The exit of Britain from India was very hasty and messy. The Imperial rule in India was marked by constant revolts and brutal suppression. The British Army managed to march out of the sub-continent without even a shot fired. There were only seven causalities. The exit was followed by the unexpected cruel bloodbath between the Hindus and Muslims. Due to the colonial invasion across the sub-continent, the communities that co-existed for almost a millennium ended up attacking each other in a terrifying outbreak of sectarian riots; with Sikhs and Hindus on one side and Muslims on the other. The riots were very intense with arson, massacres, forced conversions, sexual violence, and mass abductions. More than seventy thousand women were raped and many of them were mutilated.

Now the question arises here that how did the intermixed culture of India unravel so quickly? If we check the history, most of the polarization between Hindus and Muslims occurred during the two decades of the twentieth century and it got so worse that both sides were forced to believe that they could not live together as the two religions could not survive together.

Many historians and writers blame the British for creating this division between two nations. Based on the divide-and-rule strategy, the British started to define communities based on their religious identities. They then attached political representations to these communities. As a result, Indians were forced to ask themselves which box they belonged to.

Islam, as a religion, entered the sub-continent in the 11th century when Turks from central Afghanistan seized Delhi from its Hindu ruler. By the 13th century they had spread their rule to the other areas of the sub-continent from Gujrat to Bengal. When we look at the old Sanskrit literature, all these conquests are identified by their ethnic and linguistic affiliations (mostly "Turks") and not from their religious affiliation. However, when we see modern literature, we see that these conquests are perceived as being made by "Muslims". After the advent of Islam in the sub-continent, around one-fifth of the sub-continent's population started identifying themselves as Muslims. The Sufism became common, which was associated with spreading Islam. However, Sufi spiritualists also respected Hinduism as a religion and adopted many practices from Hinduism including: the yogic practices of Hindu sadhus, praying while hanging themselves upside down and rubbing ashes on their bodies, etc.

Throughout the sub-continent the cultural mixing took place. The Mughal crown Prince Dara Shikoh had Gita (the central text of Hinduism) translated into Persian language and then composed a study of Hinduism and Islam. Not all Mughal rulers were open-minded and peace-loving e.g. Dara's brother Aurangzeb has still not been forgotten by Hindus for his bigotry. But the last Mughal emperor clearly wrote that Islam and Hinduism "share the same essence" and his court practiced this.

Even in the 19th century, cultures, traditions and languages cut across the religious groupings in the sub-continent. People did not strongly define themselves through their religious faith. A Muslim from Bengal had a lot more common in his outlook (fondness for fish and language) with one of his Hindu co-workers than he would with a Muslim from Karachi or Sufi from North-Western part of the sub-continent. But when the British rule took over the sub-continent, religion was played as a pawn to implement the divide and rule strategy.

There is no doubt in the fact that the Muslim elites from the North Western part of the sub-continent were another force in play. The Muslim elites were neither able to accept their secondary status in the state nor were they ready to share their powers. Before the partition, the Muslim League was a strong political party in West as well as East Pakistan due to created religious segregation. However, as Pakistan emerged, the focus of the League became biased and it became an instrument of Muslim elites from the North-Western region of the sub-continent. These elites saw themselves as hires of Mughal traditions. This elite identity was quite different from the Bengali Muslim identity as Bengali Muslims were more connected to the Bengali culture which was pioneered by Hindus. The Muslim elites from West Pakistan always considered Bengali Muslims to be inferior: culturally and racially. This highlights that tensions existed within one religion as well. Since politics was connected to religious identities by the British rule, everyone got united under one religion. The creation of this religious division aided the British in preventing the collaboration between the Muslim and Hindu elites, which could have been detrimental to the British rule.

Chapter III – Independence and the Bloody Partition

In 1946, Britain gave up control of the sub-continent. Muslim representative party (Muslim League) and Hindu representative party (INC) voted for the partition of the sub-continent; based on religious separation. Finally, based on the religious division, the nations of India and Pakistan were formed.

The final Viceroy of Britain, Lord Mountbatten, flew into Delhi in March 1947. His mission was to hand over the power and to get out of the sub-continent at the earliest possibility. After a series of meetings with the Muslim League's leader: Jinnah, he was convinced that it was difficult to negotiate with Jinnah because of his stubbornness. The Viceroy was worried that if he failed at persuading all the parties for the partition of sub-continent, the Britain might end up refereeing a civil war in the sub-continent. Mountbatten ended up deploying his considerable effort in convincing other parties to agree on the partition.

The Partition

On June 3rd, Mountbatten announced his partition plan (also known as Mountbatten plan) along with the date for the transfer of powers i.e. 15th August 1947. This announcement took many people by surprise because the date was announced earlier than expected.

This might have been done in haste by Mountbatten because he witnessed the intense tensions between the two parties, and he wanted to ensure that they realized that they were moving towards sectarian heights. However, this rush exacerbated the confusion leading to chaos.

The Mountbatten's plan included the partition of Muslim-majority provinces of the Punjab and Bengal achieved the actual partition of the sub-continent into Pakistan and India. The areas with Sikh and Hindu majority were assigned to new India and the areas with Muslim-majority were assigned to Pakistan. Apart from Gandhi, many top leaders of the congress voted in favor of Partition. Ultimately, both congress and Muslim League approved the plan. At the same time, Sikhs and other communities also agreed with the plan.

The partition of sub-continent was based on the two-nation theory. The theory depicted that Hindus and Muslims were two distinct nations, apart from their cultural and linguistic commonalities. As the primary identifying factor for the Muslims of the sub-continent, was their religion which unified them. The theory advocated for a separate homeland for the Muslims in the Muslim majority areas of the sub-continent where they could practice Islam as a dominant religion. Muslim League, under the leadership of Muhammad Ali Jinnah, was the flag bearer of this ideology and Jinnah played a vital role in carving out a separate nation for Muslims. Several Hindu nationalist parties also supported the two-nation theory. They wanted to re-describe Indian Muslims as second-class citizens in India to such an extent that they wanted to call them non-Indian foreigners and they wanted to drive out the whole Muslim community out of India. The radical Hindus wanted to set up India as a Hindu state in order to restrict conversions to Islam and enforce conversion of Muslim population of India to Hinduism. On the other hand, the radical Muslims were not in favor of two-nation theory as they wanted to spread Islam in the whole sub-continent and having a separate homeland with Islam as a dominant religion restricted their Islamic preaching opportunities. In this scenario, Muslims who were in favor of this theory were seeking peace instead of favoring a religious divide. Remember! Jinnah was never in favor of partition initially. However, the circumstances of the continent pushed him to advocate for a separate country for Muslims and his vision was to create a separate land in Muslim majority area; where Muslims could practice their religion freely. At the same time, he never wanted to eradicate other religions from that part of the sub-continent. So, he preached co-existence. This was very clear from his speech at the first session of constituent assembly after Partition: *"You are free! You are free to go to your temples. You are free! Free to go to your mosque or any other place of worship. In this state of Pakistan, you may belong to any religion or caste or creed that has nothing to do with the business of the state"*. This address is a clear indication that Jinnah was never a bigot, but he realized that the ONLY way to end religious conflicts, instigated by external intervention in the sub-continent, was to get a separate homeland for Muslims. If we think critically, what else could have been the solution in the circumstances described above (throughout this book)? Partition was the best compromise made at that time in those circumstances; because if this wouldn't have been done, there could have been an intense civil war in the whole sub-continent (in the light of some predictions), because religious hatred was incubated during the British rule and it was boiling ready for eruption once the British decided to leave the sub-continent.

The British Parliament passed the Indian Independence Act 1947 on the 18th July, 1947. This act led to the partition of British India into two new countries: India bond Pakistan, discarding the British control over the princely states. The independent territory of Pakistan came into being on the 14th August 1947 and it included two regions i.e. East Pakistan (presently Bangladesh) and West Pakistan (currently Pakistan), geographically segregated by India. Muhammad Ali Jinnah became the first governor general of Pakistan. On the other hand, India became independent from the British rule on 15th August 1947 and Jawaharlal Nehru took oath as the first Prime Minister of India with Mountbatten as the first Governor General of new India. During the time of partition, Gandhi chose to stay in Calcutta and worked to avoid communal riots. He worked with newly migrated refugees.

None of the disputants were happy with the partition design. Jinnah, who succeeded in creating a new country, ended up getting a slice of India's eastern and western extremes; separated by a wide area of Indian Territory. Jinnah warned that the partition between the Punjab and Bengal would cause serious troubles in the future.

The Period of Violence

Partition was done in haste by the British rule. A British Judge: Cyril Radcliff was assigned to draw the borders of two states. He was hardly given forty days to complete this task. The present demarcation line between Pakistan and India is also famous as Radcliffe Line. This line was made public on 17th August 1947. After the announcement of the Radcliffe Line, a horrific violence period with intense communal riots and the migration of the population started. These mutinies were not predicted by any of the Indian leaders.

These barbaric incidents with the strong tendency of genocide included: eviscerating pregnant women; mutilation of victims including chopping their genitalia and limbs; hitting the heads of newborn babies against the walls; ripping babies apart in front of their mothers and exhibiting whole dead bodies and various body parts of dead people including heads, limbs, etc.

While gangs of killers were setting the whole villages on fire, hacking to death children, aged and men, while taking away women to rape them. British did not intervene where their intervention was required, by sending their troops to stop these brutalities.

Millions of people left their homeland and their properties overnight and travelled on foot, bullock carts, trains and whatever means available to the new land. Maximum number of people got displaced from Punjab province, as around 4.7 million Sikhs and Hindus migrated from West Pakistan to India and 6.5 million Muslims migrated from India to West Pakistan. On the eastern end, 2.6 million Hindus migrated to India from East Pakistan and 0.7 million Muslims migrated from India to East Pakistan. Many people died during the migration period due to the bloody massacre. Data provided by the 1931 and 1951 census revealed that around 2.23 million people went missing during migration along Punjab border which included 0.84 million Hindus/Sikhs and 1.26 million Muslims.

It took years for both India and Pakistan to resettle the refugees. Partition was a historical event in the sub-continent and this event continues to influence how states and people of South Asia envision their past, present, and future. This partition developed a complex, hostile and strenuous relationship between Pakistan and India which prevails to date.

Chapter IV – Princely States

British decided to carve the boundary of Pakistan based on the Muslim majority provinces with the boundaries determined by the Radcliffe line at the time of partition. The power transfer was only applied to the provinces that were directly ruled by the British i.e. 54% of the sub-continent's territory. The remaining 46% of the continent was ruled by the British through treaties with the local rulers of 564 states (princely states) which included: Mysore, Hyderabad, Patiala, Jammu & Kashmir, Gwalior, Udaipur, Jaipur, and Travancore. In May 1946, the Cabinet Mission Plan determined that the British supremacy over these states would be dissolved with the departure of Britain from the sub-continent and that these states would become independent. Though, many of them wanted to join India or Pakistan under a new federal relationships or political agreements.

A New Battleground

The departure of Britain from the sub-continent opened a new battleground for the Muslim League and Congress. Both of them started to try and expand the territorial boundaries of their respective countries. Both parties agreed that two-nation theory for the partition of the sub-continent would not be applied to the princely states which meant no fixed formula for allocating the princely states to the two dominions. The INC leaders had agreed on the partition of sub-continent with the condition that League would accept the division as final settlement and there would be no question of dividing or allocating princely states. Jinnah had also mentioned this during his Lahore resolution address that the demand for a separate dominion is confined to the British India. Lahore resolution, prepared and written by Muhammad Zafar Ullah Khan mentioned:

"That geographically contiguous units are demarcated regions which should be constituted, with such territorial readjustments as may be necessary that the areas in which the Muslims are numerically in a majority as in the North Western and Eastern Zones of (British) India should be grouped to constitute 'independent states' in which the constituent units should be autonomous and sovereign".

Muslim League kept approaching all the princely states in order to persuade them to either join Pakistan or to be independent, irrespective of their Muslim or Hindu character.

On the other hand, INC did not want to lose any more territory on account of two-nation theory. Nehru agreed that the princely states would be free to join either Pakistani or Indian Constituent Assembly, but his government did not agree to recognize the right of princely states to independence. Hence, in April 1947, he declared that "any state which did not come into the Constituent Assembly will be considered as a hostile state and such state will have to bear consequences". Congress realized the importance of situation and prioritized the accession of princely states into the Indian Territory.

Referring to Kashmir, Patiala, and Bahawalpur, Jinnah made it very clear that if these states willingly agreed to join Pakistan, they would be welcomed with an honorable and reasonable settlement. However, he also emphasized that the League had no desire to coerce or force them into any agreement.
British agreed on the establishment of Pakistan but after the partition line was disclosed, Jinnah was not happy with the

partition, but he failed to expand Pakistan's territories within British India. In order to increase the size of Pakistan, two groups were targeted: The Princes and the Sikh community. Since the two-sided communal violence during the partition had led to the increased conflicts among Muslims and Sikhs; therefore, the other way of expanding the boundaries of Pakistan was by persuading princely states or by limiting the number of princely states joining India. Jinnah still supported and respected the right to independence of the princely states, and he supported the British proposal for ending their paramountcy.

He stated: "Legally and constitutionally, Indian princely states will be independent states after the dissolution of paramountcy, and they will be free to decide whatever course they want to take. It is up to them if they want to join Pakistan Constituent Assembly or India Constituent Assembly or they want to remain completely independent. In case, they want to stay independent, they will have to get into an agreement with either Pakistan or India based on their choice."

League was sure that this was a win-win deal as Jinnah believed that he had princely states within the boundaries of Pakistan, and he was confident about his negotiation skills. Therefore, the league did not focus on initiating serious negotiations until the transfer of power. Another issue was that there were more princely states in India than Pakistan therefore, India faced a greater potential of princely states' declaration of independence than Pakistan.

The Autonomy of Princely States

If princely states decided to be independent that would have been at the cost of India and not of Pakistan. Therefore, INC was a bit concerned about this issue. Among all the princely states, Travancore: the southernmost state of India - despite being surrounded by India on three sides, was the first state to declare that it would become independent. Jinnah had a long meeting with the ruler of this state during late 1947. Later, Hyderabad decided to follow similar path. The League was very flexible regarding the independence of princely states. *Dawn,* the famous newspaper in Pakistan, reported: "There are a lot of differences between the approach of Muslim League and Congress in regard to the matter of princely states.

League has promised to NOT intervene and be flexible that it would not be a surprise if a number of even non-Muslim states decide to either completely join Pakistan Constituent Assembly or be in close relations with Pakistan as compared to India. The princely states, as an autonomous member of Pakistan or as allies of Pakistan, will have a more respectful position than otherwise. Congress has been threatening these states for so long and there is no doubt that Hyderabad and Travancore will stand up to and refuse to be bullied. They can be an example for those states that have not made their minds up yet."

According to some historians, convincing princely states to stay independent was his strategy to weaken India and stop masses of the population to join India. Jinnah tried to convince some Hindu rulers to border Rajput states to stay independent and then join Pakistan later on terms dictated by the ruler of the states. However, ambiguity existed, i.e. whether it was Jinnah's strategy or his respect for the right to independence of the princely states.

Muslim League also agreed to accept the accession of Jungarah, where 85% of the population was Hindus and it did not share any borders with Pakistan. This also indicated that Jinnah favored co-existence (as mentioned in the last section). Hence, the matter of princely states was not about ideology, but it was more about expanding the geographical reach of Pakistan; while respecting the rights of the princely states.

Chapter V – Kashmir

After the invasion in the 19th century, Britain sold the entire Kashmir Valley to the repressive ruler of Jammu: Hindu Gulab Singh (Dogras), under the Treaty of Amritsar signed in 1846. It was under Singh's rule that Kashmir Valley became a part of the princely state Jammu and Kashmir. Kashmir remained an independent princely state until 1947.

Demography and Composition

The Kashmiris were predominantly Muslims, but they were ruled by Hindu maharaja. The rule was completely blind to the underlying cultural, socioeconomic, ethnic and regional affinities of Kashmiris. This played a huge role in changing the path of the politics in Kashmir. Religious ideology was mixed up with politics and power was used to repress the religion which was in the majority but not in power.

Singh's rule was famous for strong religious bias against Muslims and regional bias against Kashmiris. People belonging to the Kashmir region were not allowed to possess arms. Muslims were excluded from state services, they were heavily taxed, and business and trade were monopolized. Muslims were also restricted to pursue quality and modern education and that shunned their chances to progress. This repression led to distrust in Hindu rule. However, polarization in Kashmir was not merely the result of ethno-religious suppression of Kashmiris or Muslims only. It also evolved as a result of state patronage system which led to the deprivation of the indigenous population of their economic, religious, and political rights. Muslims in

Kashmir complained about the Pandits: the indigenous inhabitants of Kashmir Valley, that they filled all the ranks in the state administration leaving Muslims behind and at the bottom ring of the society. On the other hand, the Pandits also highlighted that the Dogras have formed their army and put the top posts aside for their own people (Dogras) in the state bureaucracy.

Kashmiri Muslims were also divided into small groups based on their political interests. Educated young Muslims in Srinagar formed a reading room party to secure quality education and jobs in state administration. Muslims who worked in silk factory were focused on better working condition and the Muslim Young Men League in Jammu was busy in hidden activities to achieve political and economic independence of the state.

The Agitation

The early agitation that took place due to the political activities was limited in its scope and purpose until the Dogra, Maharaja of the state, waged in a massive Muslim agitation in 1931. This agitation was called a religious war and this war was a turning point in enhancing the differences between the Muslims and non-Muslims (Kashmiri Pandits and Dogra Hindus) of Jammu and Kashmir. Pandits also supported Dogra rule when this war broke out. When Glancy Commission was appointed by Maharaja of the state to address the issues of Muslims, Pandits opposed that. Later, the Kashmiri Pandits Movement lost its momentum and ceased to exist as a political force. In 1932, Kashmiri Muslims united under all Jammu and Kashmir Conference and demanded: a bigger share in the civil services for educated young Muslims, better working conditions for laborers working in the industry, land ownership, and Muslims recruitment in the army. Other demands included religious demands i.e. the removal of obstructions to the conversion of Hindus to Islam and return of the mosques to the Muslim community. This struggle, of Kashmiri Muslim Leaders, was supported by other Muslims in the sub-continent.

When Maharaja of Jammu and Kashmir used his power to suppress this movement, the leaders of Kashmiri Muslims asked Muslims to pick up the arms against the authority by participating in his processions. Thousands of Muslims picked up the arms and congregated at Khanyar, Srinagar. Seeing that the situation was getting out of control, the Maharaja asked for help from the British military. He informed the British government that an armed revolt had broken out in Jammu and Kashmir. The British intervention in the state's matters revealed that the princely states were serving the interest of the British rule rather than Maharaja and that it was only an instrument of the colonial power run by Maharaja. So, the people of the state realized that their political freedom was directly linked to the paramountcy of the British rule rather than Maharaja's ethnic and religious background. After this realization, Kashmiri Muslims put aside their religion and emerged as a new regional and secular entity. Many local political organizations emerged with the nationalist, secular outlook and socialist objectives. These liberal movements allowed the Kashmiri leaders to look at the conflict from a different perspective and they stopped focusing on the religious roots of the conflicts. Rather, they focused on the manipulative nature of the state's economic and political structures.

The Kashmir's Muslim Conference approached INC with an intention to have INC as an ally as INC was also focused on the agenda of getting rid of British rule. Despite its secular nature,

Kashmir's Muslim Conference was engaged in the communally oriented political movement and INC denied getting involved in that. Therefore, Congress suggested the Muslim leaders from Kashmir transform Muslim Conference into a national organization.

In 1939, during a special session, the Muslim Conference was converted into All Jammu and Kashmir National Conference. The National Conference went beyond the demands of welfare improvements for Muslims only. It started to seek for the restricted economic and political system of the state of Jammu and Kashmir. This was also highlighted in their Naya Kashmir manifesto which was released in 1944.

The National Conference kept coordinating its efforts at a national level, aligning its activities with the popular political movements across the country. The leaders of the National Conference knew that the revolt in princely states was not as much against the Princes but the British colonial power. Also, they were aware that Kashmiri's could not stand up alone against this colonial power. Therefore, it was important to get involved in the political movements at the national level.

The National Conference demanded liquidation of the Dogra rule, dissolution of the British paramountcy and repudiation of the Treaty of Amritsar. The leadership of the Conference regarded the princely system as a strategic game by the British rule and National Conference's "Quit Kashmir" movement was considered as an extension of the overall Indian struggle for freedom from British rule.

'Quit Kashmir' movement was strongly opposed by the Maharaja. He decided to destroy the movement by using his power. People involved in agitation and rebellion against Dogra rule were either arrested or shot. Outside Kashmir, Nehru from INC supported the Quit Kashmir movement and asked many political organizations to hold processions and meetings to show their solidarity with Kashmiris.

On the other hand, a section of the Muslim Conference leadership had strong constraints regarding the shift towards a secular political system and resisted the transformation of the Muslim Conference into the National Conference. These leaders were based in the Jammu region. In their view, the transformation of Muslim Conference into a more secular entity would divide the Muslims. According to these leaders, the Hindus would never cooperate, not even with the secular party because they had their interest tied up with Dogra rule. Also, Congress being a Hindu dominant party would support Hindus instead of supporting Muslims in a state ruled by Hindus.

One of the leaders from the Muslim Conference in Kashmir, Choudhary Ghulam Abbas, stood up against the idea of national unity and declared that Muslims and Hindus were two separate nations and integration was not possible. Other leaders also agreed on reorganizing the Muslim Conference with separate electorates and addressed the grievances of Muslims in the economic, political and administrative issues. With this reorganization, many Muslim leaders from Mirpur, Poonch, and Kotli areas of the state of Jammu and Kashmir decided to break away. After breaking away, they along with Azad Muslim Conference (another party within Kashmir region) established a local unit of Muslim League which was based in Srinagar.

National Conference continued to struggle. The more the National Conference focused on secular politics, the more it came closer to the National Congress. The two parties continued to support each other until the Pakistan resolution in 1940. At this time the National Conference was split as many Muslim leaders in Mirpur, Poonch and Muzaffarabad supported the demand for a separate homeland for the Muslims of sub-continent. The National Conference broke and the Muslim Conference was formally revived in 1941.

The demands of the Muslim Conference included: restitution of land rights, removal of law that restricted cow slaughtering, representation of the Muslims in the civil services, retraction of the Arms Act and amendment in the Personal Law of inheritance of Hindus. Furthermore, the members of Muslim Conference wanted the transfer of political power to the political leadership representing the majority of the population in the state i.e. the Muslim Conference.

Free Kashmir, also known as Azad Kashmir, issued a manifesto in 1945 and committed that Muslims of Jammu and Kashmir would join Muslim League in their efforts for a separate homeland. They supported Jinnah and united for one objective i.e. the realization of Pakistan.

The Muslim Conference also opposed the "Quit India" movement instigated by National Conference. According to the Muslim Conference, the "Quit India" movement was a conspiracy that National Conference designed in union with Congress to divide the Muslims and promote Hindu rule in the state. Later on "Direct Action": a civil disobedience movement was launched by Muslim Conference on request of the Muslim League. Due to this movement, many leaders from Muslim Conference ended up behind the bars. Internal differences and conflicts among the acting leaders of Muslim Conference began to brew and its activities came to a halt.

On the other side, the leaders behind the bars kept sending agitated messages to the party asking for recommencement of the disobedience movement. Nonetheless, instead of resuming the movement Jinnah was approached by the acting leaders of the party to stop the agitation. The civil disobedience movement ended. However, it left the party divided and influenced the authority of the party in the state of Jammu and Kashmir.

Maharaja of the state of Jammu and Kashmir also used a divide-and-rule strategy to strengthen his rule in the state. One of the examples of this strategy was: passing a special ordinance for introducing two different scripts in the government schools of the state i.e. Persian and Devanagari. This ordinance along with the Arms Act of 1940 (which prohibited everyone apart from Dogras to possess arm in the state) flared up the Muslim leaders in the National Conference and they started to pit against their Hindu colleagues.

The friction between the Hindus and Muslims in the National Conference widened when the Muslim leaders from the National Conference approached and started negotiations with Jinnah and Muslim Conference in 1943. Jinnah visited Kashmir. He called for unity amongst Muslims by highlighting that Muslims from India were supporting the cause of the two-nation theory and an independent land for Muslims. Jinnah's powerful words, during his speech in Kashmir, further created a rift in the National Conference as a political entity. Jinnah calmly asked the Muslim leaders from the National Conference to unite with the Muslim Conference and the Muslim members of both parties to merge.

This also meant that the Muslim leadership of the National Conference would have to give up everything for which they fought. One key Muslim leader from the National Conference, Sheikh Abdullah, refused to unite. Hence, National Conference gave up on the idea of collaborating with Muslim League. Jinnah realized that it would be impossible to win plebiscite without convincing Abdullah.

Serious ideological differences started brewing within the National Conference. It was not only Muslims against Non-Muslims but Muslims against Muslims, where conservatives opposed Congress's ideas. Despite all these differences, the party managed to stay together. This was primarily because of the Sikh and Hindu leaders who knew that National Conference provided them with an outstanding political platform and therefore, it was important for them to strengthen Muslim force with liberal views in order to promote a secular political cause in the party. They also realized that quitting would only put them at the risk of being reduced to a minority in the state's politics.

Kashmir's Geographic Placement

After the decision of sub-continent's partition into India and Pakistan, Kashmir became immensely important. The state of Jammu and Kashmir was not only the largest princely state in India but its geographical placement made it unique; as it shared borders with China, Afghanistan, and the Soviet Socialist Republic along with being a part of carvan trade route from Central Asia to India.

It was very important to control Kashmir for both India and Pakistan given its political, strategic and economic importance. Securing Kashmir also meant securing defensible borders.

The sub-continent had a history of invasions from the northwest. Therefore, Pakistan also feared an invasion from India if India managed to take over Jammu and Kashmir. Pakistan, being concerned about its security, applied its military-strategic logic. According to this logic, if Kashmir's western part became Pakistan-India, border it would lay very close to the rail and road network between the cities of Lahore and Rawalpindi, making the chances of invasion highly disastrous for the newly established Pakistan. Many researchers and historians have mentioned that Pakistan supported a tribal invasion into the western end of Kashmir, in 1947, which was led by military General Akbar Khan. According to Khan, after looking at the map of Pakistan, it becomes very obvious that the military security of the country would be seriously threatened if the Indian troops get stationed along the western border of Kashmir. He also mentioned that this would have exposed Pakistanis to a risky situation where independence could never be a reality.

Kashmir held vital importance for the agricultural economy of Pakistan as the four rivers of West Pakistan (i.e. The Indus, Chenab, Jhelum, and Ravi) originated from the mountain ranges of Jammu and Kashmir. The rivers ran across West Punjab, whose progress was dependent on irrigation. Hence, Kashmir was an absolute necessity for Pakistan for its independent existence.

The strategic and economic realities, along with the Muslim League's and Congress's ideological justification for including Kashmir in either Pakistan or India, were modified after partition.

Maharaja and his People

Congress was supporting the struggle of Kashmiris against the Dogra rule. Also, it backed the position of National Conference by advocating that the political future of the state must be decided by its people. Right after the partition, Congress asked the maharaja to determine the will of his people and join either

India or Pakistan. Congress, certainly, didn't want the state of Jammu and Kashmir to be Independent as that would have extreme ramifications for Indian unity. Indian 1st Deputy Prime Minister, Sardar Patel, mentioned that he was ready to leave the decision to the ruler of the state. If the ruler felt that his state's and his interest laid in joining Pakistan then India would not stand in their way. The Maharaja asked for a Stand-still agreement in order to get some time to make a final decision on the political status of Kashmir. However, India did not agree to sign such an agreement. It wanted to examine the implications of such an agreement in detail as India was privy to the internal problems and situation of the state because of the population composition. On the other hand, Congress did not push Maharaja to join Indian territory.

Similarly, Pakistan's interest in Kashmir was not very evident. Kashmir was never seen as an integral part of Pakistan's conception as a separate nation. The question here is that if Kashmir was always considered as a part of Pakistan's conception, then why Muslim League along with the Muslim Conference did not ask the Maharaja of the state to join Pakistan and instead they promised full subsistence and support if he declared independence. Some historians argue that Jinnah had no interest in Kashmir and he took Kashmir for granted. He thought that the idea of Pakistan as a separate homeland would automatically influence the state as it influenced the rest of the sub-continent but the political situation in Kashmir was very complex.

After partition the National Conference asked for common people, not the princes, to represent the state of Jammu and Kashmir in the Indian Constituent Assembly. Once the Congress accepted the decision of partition, the dream of united

India was shattered. As a result of this decision, the members of the National Conference demanded the transfer of power from the Dogra Maharajas to the people of the state, before joining India. Therefore, their slogan became: *"Freedom before accession"*. The personal choice of National Conference's leader, Sheikh Abdullah, was very vague as he opposed the partition between India and Pakistan but at the same time, he did not want to join the Indian Constituent Assembly.

According to his predictions, Pakistan would not accept the decision of the state to accede to India and Kashmir would become a battle-ground. He also recognized that existing as an independent state between two powerful countries was not possible.

The Muslim Conference was more focused on collaboration with the Maharaja in order to persuade him to declare independence for Kashmir. The support and cooperation from the Muslims of Kashmir, who were 80% of the state's population, was promised by the leaders of the Muslim Conference. They also assured that the Muslims would continue to recognize him as the ruler, i.e. the first constitutional king of the democratic state. Muslim Conference had this understanding that Kashmir was a Muslim majority state and Maharaja would be ultimately forced to either hand over or at least share his powers with Muslims.

Maharaja knew that his decision of either acceding to Pakistan or to India would make him lose anyway. Kashmir's linkage with Pakistan and India in terms of culture, society, economy, and geography made the decision difficult. Most of all, this decision was putting Maharaja's political future at stake. If the state was to accede to India, the National conference along with Congress could have asked him to surrender as they were fighting his regime for a long time. His own Dogra Hindu community would get endangered if the state was to accede to Pakistan. After all these considerations, Maharaja preferred independence because independence would allow him to maintain his authority and political control over the state. Britain and Congress warned Maharaja that declaring independence was not a good choice but he disregarded all those warnings. Additionally, he failed to realize that Kashmir as an independent state would be very vulnerable to military and political coercion from either side (India or Pakistan).

In order to gain some additional time to finalize his decision, he sought a Standstill Agreement with both Pakistan and India. The Agreement specified that all administrative and other arrangements on the matters of common concern between Kashmir and other Indian states should continue as they were, until new arrangements in this regard were agreed on. This meant that the central government of both India and Pakistan would have no authority over Kashmir, for that time. The agreement was signed by Pakistan, but India did not sign the agreement.

Chapter VI – The Game

Everything changed when the Britain transferred power after partition. The Prime Minister: R.C. Kak, who had promised Kashmir to the Pakistani politicians, was dismissed by the Maharaja of the state of Jammu and Kashmir. Kak was also reported to have been deciding Kashmir's future by considering the possibility of holding a referendum. After his dismissal, Pakistan's calculations regarding Kashmir were endangered. Muslim League and Muslim Conference started to pursue efforts of collaboration with Maharaja but did not gain people's support. These efforts were the result of the realization that 'people did not matter to Maharaja' after he dismissed the Prime Minister. It was believed that collaboration with Maharaja might help lead to the voices of the people of Kashmir. As a result of this situation, none of the parties were sure about the results of the referendum.

After the partition and independence, the strategy of the Muslim League and Muslim Conference changed from independence for the state to accession to Pakistan. Pakistan pressed that Kashmir was a Muslim majority state and its accession to Pakistan was the integral idea of the Pakistani nation. However, this idea never came into light before that time.

The Revolt

While these matters were still unsolved, a revolt broke out in Poonch against Dogra forces and armed informal soldiers via Pakistan entered Poonch, Muzaffarabad, and Mirpur. Pakistan cut off all the supplies entering Kashmir by rail and road in order to control the situation of revolt. Later in October 1947, irregular soldiers and armed tribesmen occupied Kashmir.

The raiders were not formally sent by Pakistan, but they entered via Pakistan. However, instead of acceding to Pakistan, Maharaja released the leaders of the National Conference and requested help from the Indian military to deal with the attack of raiders and finally decided to accede to India. After this decision, the Indian government sent troops to Jammu in order to fight raiders off.

The Muslim Conference had strong presence and support in the border areas of Jammu i.e. Poonch, Muzaffarabad and Mirpur and their people also supported accession to Pakistan. The tribal raiders were welcomed by the people of these areas for revolting against the Dogra forces. However, the revolt in Poonch did not instigate revolt in overall Kashmir because National Conference also had a strong presence in Kashmir valley, and they were not in favor of the two nation theory.

India also had strong stakes in Kashmir and therefore they were not ready to accept Kashmir's accession to Pakistan. They were fully prepared to drive Pakistani forces out of Kashmir and to do everything possible to incorporate Kashmir into the Indian dominion.

A Flashpoint between Pakistan and India

The fate of Kashmir was not decided, and it remained a fighting ground throughout the year 1948. Reversing Kashmir's accession to India became the primary agenda of Pakistan. At this point, Indian leaders also started using this opportunity to validate their point. Nehru began to see the issue of Kashmir through the ideological lens and highlighted that Kashmir would be a real demonstration of secularism in India and Muslims all around the world would witness that.

Once the state of Kashmir joined India the agenda of Congress changed. It shifted from the geographical merging of the Indian state to shaping the political character. Nehru was the principal designer behind this change. According to Nehru, including Kashmir in the Indian territory was central in justifying his modernist ideology regarding secular and plural India. Voluntary decision by a Muslim-majority state, the state of Jammu and Kashmir, supported Nehru's ideology. According to Nehru, if Kashmir would have decided to join Pakistan or to stay independent, it could have had led to communal hatred between Hindus and Muslims leading to nurturing disputative tendencies in India.

Nehru decided to take Kashmir's issue to the United Nations and he offered to hold a plebiscite to decide the future of Kashmir but later on, he changed his mind. In one of the radio broadcasts Nehru promised that the people of Kashmir would decide the future of Kashmir and a referendum, managed by United Nations, would be held for this purpose. This announcement was also aligned with the long-held agenda of Congress. In November 1947, Jinnah was approached by the governor general of India: Lord Mountbatten. He proposed plebiscite for the three remaining states i.e. Hyderabad, Kashmir, and Junagarh. However, Jinnah refused this proposal.

Nehru never wanted accession of the state of Jammu and Kashmir to be decided by the ruler of the state. However, later on his views changed and he developed the view that it was essential to convince Maharaja to agree on accession in order to fully establish India's power over Kashmir. On the other hand, a plebiscite would only secure what was popular. The offer to hold plebiscite was retracted and it had a lot to do with the political circumstances.

Nehru did not want to lose Kashmir at any cost and Maharaja also requested Indian help to drive out raiders from Kashmir. Therefore, the military was sent to the state of Kashmir and the purpose of sending the army was not only to deal with the issue of raiders but also to predict the involvement of Pakistan's army and to make nationalist political forces strong. Nehru also had an opinion on tribal raiders that they had full support from Pakistan and that Pakistan strategized this invasion as an informal military move in Kashmir to create disruption and pressurize the Maharaja to join Pakistan. However, this opinion was never validated with evidence, so the argument remained weak.

Jinnah had different views. He told Lord Mountbatten that with the presence of Indian troops and the strong influence of National Conference, average Muslims would be suppressed, and they would find it difficult to vote for Pakistan.

Although the invading tribesmen were losing ground, Nehru was not satisfied with the military response from India. According to him, Pakistan strategized a small-scale regular war with the latest weapons via supporting raiders and the response from Indian army was only defensive. He wanted the military to attack all the bases of invaders along with the communication lines in West Punjab and Frontier Province of Pakistan. This enhanced the risk of a war between the two dominions. Seeing this, Mountbatten convinced Nehru to involve the United Nations to settle the issue.

United Nations' Intervention & Plebiscite

Kashmir's issue took an ideological turn when it was referred to the United Nations. On January 1948, a letter was written to United Nations Security Council by Nehru. He mentioned Pakistan is providing aid to the invaders for operations against Jammu and Kashmir (a State which acceded to the Dominion of India). Nehru requested the council to call upon Pakistan to end the acts of aggression against India.

Pakistan responded to India's claims with their own letter to the United Nations Security Council by rejecting India's claim and explaining other grievances regarding India's conduct. Pakistan also highlighted that the invading tribesmen were not armed by Pakistan, but they were local rebels who stood up against Maharaja when he decided to accede to the India and they were being crushed by Indian army. The prime minister of Pakistan, Liaquat Ali Khan, mentioned that Kashmir's accession to India was fraudulent and was a method to show aggression towards Pakistan to undo the newly established dominion. Pakistan also mentioned that this case will be presented to the council by its first foreign minister Sir Mohammed Zafarullah Khan.

Sir Zafarullah Khan first called upon India to stop its aggression in Kashmir and to implement the partition agreements and second, to appoint a commission which can investigate the charge of genocide, arrange evacuation, and work on cease fire in Kashmir.

He further mentioned that the latter would entail the withdrawal of outsiders (either from Pakistan or India); steps for establishment of an impartial and independent administration; and a plebiscite to ensure that the people of Kashmir can exercise free and autonomous will, irrespective of whether the state decides to accede to Pakistan or India.

According to one of the articles in The Daily Times, Sir Zafarullah Khan's presentation of Kashmir case to the United Nations was also acknowledged by the Indian democrats. He also emphasized, "it would be the duty of the plebiscite administrator to establish the conditions which would ensure and grantee that the plebiscite is in every respect free and impartial".

After presenting this issue at the global platform, the United Nations, Britain and later Americans supported Pakistan. According to them, acceding to Pakistan was better for Kashmir and this was considered as a huge victory of Pakistan at a global platform. This time, the tables turned, not because of Pakistan but because of the international support. Some historians call it a conspiracy from the British, but history still has to prove the role of British in derailing the solution of Kashmir conflict and its preservation.

British Commonwealth Relations Officer, by pursuing a diplomatic course, asked India to undo all the military and political gains achieved in Kashmir. India appealed but its argument about the invading tribesmen supported by Pakistan was ignored by the Security Council.

British proposals, to the Security Council and its allies, in February 1948 had put Pakistan and India on the same moral footholds. They also asked for the removal of National Conference and Maharaja's rule in the state and suggested that Kashmir's administration should be taken over by a United Nation-appointed administration. The proposals also included allowing Pakistan to replace the tribal invaders with the regular army and take control over the Muslim dominant part of the state and allowing India to take control of the Hindu dominant parts of the state.

United Nations Commission formalized its resolution on 13th August 1948 as: *"Question of the accession of the State of Jammu and Kashmir to India or Pakistan will be decided through the democratic method of a free and impartial plebiscite: a plebiscite will be held when it shall be found by the Commission that the ceasefire and truce agreements set forth in the parts I and II (regarding the ceasefire and withdrawal of Pakistani troops in the State of Jammu and Kashmir, respectively) of the Commission's Resolution of 13 August 1948 have been carried out and arrangements for the plebiscite have been completed; the Secretary-General of theUnited Nations will in agreement with the commission, nominate a "plebiscite administrator" who shall be personality of high international standing and commanding general confidence."*

India considered this proposal as a one-sided approach and therefore, regarded the United Nations as a biased institution for years. Nehru approached the United Nations to ensure fair play with the help of their presence during the Plebiscite but later he ended up complaining about the United Nations for encroaching India's rights in Kashmir and empowering Pakistan.

To elaborate on plebiscite, United Nations Commission laid out another proposal for the state of Jammu and Kashmir. The proposal stated: *"... .the question of accession to India or Pakistan" was to be decided by a free and impartial plebiscite, which was contingent upon having a case-fire. The two countries accepted the cease-fire plan and allowed the UN to observe the ceasefire from 1 January 1949. The ceasefire line "went through the western part of Jammu and the eastern part of Poonch, leaving the capital city of Poonch on the Indian side of the line, then crossed the Jhelum River at a point west of Uri and made a large sweep following the valley of the Kishinganga River. From there, it proceeded to Kargil, which also remained on the Indian side, and then north-west to the Chinese border. Hunza, Gilgit, Baltistan, Chilas, the great part of Poonch, and the smaller part of Jammu remained in control of Pakistan and Azad Kashmir."*

The division of Jammu and Kashmir took place after the cease-fire which was declared on 1st January 1949. The state got divided into two parts. Half of the state including the Jammu region, Ladakh and Kashmir Valley joined India. The other half i.e. Poonch, Muzaffarabad, and Mirpur along with Gilgit and Baltistan were included in Pakistan. At this point, Kashmir became a constant topic of argument and tension between Pakistan and India.

United Nations, despite their intervention, was not able to broker any agreement as to how to ensure demilitarization in Kashmir or how to conduct a plebiscite. Pakistan was unwilling to draw its forces due to the possibility that India might attempt to seize Kashmir using violence and fraud based on the history of how India dealt with the issue. Therefore, Pakistan insisted upon more details on the plebiscite as to how and will that be held.

India on the other had took a strong position on Kashmir's voluntary accession to India considering only what Maharaja wanted to deal with the situation at that time. India wanted United Nations to force Pakistan to withdraw, refused to call their forces back, and remained dormant on the need of holding a plebiscite as they thought that it was not important.

From 1947 till 1954 India's official policy included plebiscite in Kashmir. However, in late 1948, Nehru started becoming skeptical of plebiscite's realization. In short, neither Pakistan nor India wanted to hold a plebiscite in Kashmir until they were sure of winning it. India did not want to rely on United Nations as it did not agree to the terms which the United Nations was trying to set for the plebiscite. On the other hand, Jinnah did not have enough support from Kashmir to expect its accession to Pakistan because Pakistan did not have support from Sheikh Abdullah and he could not be eradicated from the picture.

Sheikh Abdullah, being a leader of the National Conference, had strong hold in Kashmir Valley. However, the areas of Poonch, Muzaffarabad, and Mirpur supported Muslim Conference. The National Conference did not have a hold on Northern Territories: Hunza and Gilgit. Therefore, later Sheikh Abdullah became more inclined towards the partition of the state of Jammu and Kashmir.

The Blame Game & Continuous Tensions

The blame game did not subside for decades. Pakistan kept blaming India for breaching the pledge made to the world, the United Nations and most of all the Kashmiri people. India blamed Pakistan for not vacating Azad Kashmir first as obligated by the United Nations resolutions. The plebiscite option reached a deadlock!

After that point, India changed its strategy and tried countering Muslim Leagues' argument of "common religious affinities" with "political rights for Kashmiris". According to Nehru, he was in favor of 'inclusionary' rather than 'exclusionary' means of integration. Nehru started creating political stakes for the people of Jammu and Kashmir as an encouragement to stay with India. The right of self-determination in the state of Jammu and

Kashmir was then promised by Nehru. After making this promise, Nehru tried to balance the power struggle between Maharaja and National Conference in the state of Jammu and Kashmir. He forced Maharaja to appoint Sheikh Abdullah as the Prime Minister of the state's interim government. At the same time, Nehru strongly condemned the Praja Parishad's (a political party based on the RSS Hindu nationalist ideology) movement launched in Jammu to demand complete integration of Jammu and Kashmir with India. Nehru regarded this movement as objectionable, anti-social and against secularism principles and hence, this movement was against the basic principles on which the state of India was built.

Nehru also took the constitutional route to grant Kashmir a special status under Article 370 of the Indian constitution. This situation was unique to Jammu and Kashmir in the Indian dominion. This article defined that the residents of the state of Jammu and Kashmir live under a separate set of laws including ownership of property, citizenship and other fundamental rights as compared to the residents of other Indian states. According to this instrument of accession, the Indian Parliament gained control in the matters of foreign affairs, defense, communications and rest of the powers vested in the state.

This article also allowed Kashmir to retain its crucial cultural symbols like the separate flag and political titles i.e. 'Sadar-e-Riyasat' as opposed to the governor and 'Wazir-e-Azam' instead of Chief Minister.

In the opening speech to the Jammu and Kashmir Constituent Assembly, Sheikh Abdullah made it clear that India's nature was far more compatible with the vision of Naya Kashmir (New Kashmir) as compared to Pakistan. Therefore, the National Conference decided to accede to India.

According to Abdullah, Pakistan's most prominent argument regarding Kashmir was that 'Pakistan is a Muslim country and large chunk of Kashmir's population is Muslim and therefore there exist strong ties between Pakistan and Kashmir'. Abdullah claimed that this argument was camouflage and a political strategy to fool the common man. He was of the view that religious affinities alone should not determine the ties between the states.

One crucial weakness in the political relationship between the state of Kashmir and India was that the conception of Kashmir's autonomous status on both sides differed significantly. India viewed Jammu and Kashmir as a part of its nation. On the other hand, the Kashmiri leadership viewed the autonomous status as a co-equal position and complete internal sovereignty. Nehru was ready to grant special autonomy to Kashmir but not at the cost of the Indian state.

Therefore, whenever the political goals of the state of Jammu and Kashmir conflicted with the Indian dominion, the preference was given to the later. For example, when Kashmir's leadership opposed the strategy of merging Indian army with the state's forces, the center rejected the demand and opposed it. Soon Kashmir's leadership started perceiving the central government's pressures on various political issues as a violation of the Kashmir's autonomy. Realizing that the political aspirations set by the National Conference for Kashmir could not be met while remaining within the Indian dominion, Sheikh Abdullah started advocating for a completely independent Kashmir. This demand brought serious conflicts between Kashmir and the center as this demand had challenged India's sovereignty.

Kashmir was a test case of India's secularism. India's leadership never accepted the Two Nations Theory and the Muslim dominant state of Jammu and Kashmir did not accede to Pakistan. However, technically this case did not work because Kashmir's leadership kept arguing for complete autonomy and during this time Hindu nationalists in India got a chance to legitimize their argument that Muslims were disloyal to India.

In 1964, Abdullah accepted that Kashmir had acceded to India and India has the right to control Kashmir in the matters of external affairs, defense and communications but the rest of the sovereignty and final decision on accession will depend on the plebiscite. This statement was followed by a proposal for settlement negotiation suggestion which was well received by Nehru.

After the sudden death on Nehru in May 1964, the prospects of settlement faded, and Abdullah completely refused to accept any constitutional relationship between India and the state of Jammu and Kashmir. In order to guarantee Kashmir's rights, he also started to insist on intervention by Pakistan which was unacceptable to the central government of India. Taking in account this scenario and potential of Pakistan's involvement in the matter, the center reverted to the old policies of indulging in the political matters of the state of Jammu and Kashmir and a misconstrued version of India's national interest was used as an excuse to destabilize the democratic institutions of Kashmir. In order to bring political integration, National Congress was dissolved by the center and it was replaced by Congress.

Hence, the claim of Indian secularism turned out to be a facade that was used as a political strategy to carefully persuade Kashmir into the Indian dominion. Once engulfed, Kashmiris were denied their political right and fair share in the state-sponsored and center aided developments. This left them in despair.

Seeing their autonomy eroding, the people of Kashmir started supporting Abdullah's demand for an independent Kashmir. On the other hand, even in this scenario, the option of Joining Pakistan was not very popular.

In 1965, Pakistani troops invaded the Kashmir Valley to attack India's position in Poonch, Tithwal, and Uri. Indian forces while conducting a holding operation in Kashmir also crossed the border and launched an attack on Lahore and Sialkot. The Indian aim was not only to defend its territory in Kashmir but also to capture two main cities in Pakistan. However, after the ceasefire agreement, the military was called back, and the two sides agreed to stop the war. During the Indo-Pak war in 1965, the United Nations passed a resolution, with strong words, to agree on a cease-fire. However, the cease-fire occurred due to the intense pressure applied by the two superpowers i.e. The Unites States of America (USA) and the Soviet Union.

On the other side, Congress and National Congress remained in conflict with each other for more than a decade. This was often described as a clash between India and Kashmir. This situation forced the Muslim identity to pop out among Kashmiris and nurture loyalties with Pakistan and this posed a strong threat to the Indian state in the longer run.

Before 1986, the National Conference had fought against the domination of the center and perceived Congress as an authoritarian and oppressing party. In 1986, when National Conference joined hands with Congress, people of Kashmir felt betrayed and out of their discontent, they were forced to take an extreme approach and pursued fundamentalist outlets.

A coalition of Islamic groups, called the Muslim United Front (MUF), mobilized the Muslim identity in the 1987 elections. Kashmiri youth joined this coalition in bulk and most of these young people were from rich class and well-established business groups in Kashmir. However, the elections turned out to be unfair and rigged by the center.

The consistent and forced erosion of Kashmir's political autonomy, consecutive rulers decided by the center and manipulation of the state's electoral process led to undermining of the basic principles for accession to India. Kashmiris started to believe that they would remain marginalized like that forever and they started to demand secession which led to violent revolts in Kashmir.

All these young people, out of discontent, were convinced that the bullet will deliver where the ballot had failed; and within the jails and police control rooms, the first generation of militants was born. According to the Kashmiris, they had no option apart from picking up the guns. These young people joined Jammu and Kashmir Liberation Front (JKLF), a militant organization that operated in Azad Kashmir, Pakistan. Youth crossed the line of control and got training and arms in the camps based in Azad Kashmir. From there, JKLF established its base in Indian-controlled Kashmir.

JKLF led an underground movement to secure the independence of Kashmir which usually used violence to achieve immediate political objectives.

New Delhi was well aware of the underground militant *Azadi* (independence) movement but did not understand the urgency of dealing with it. This allowed militancy to dig deeper and strengthen roots in the state of Jammu and Kashmir.

In 1990, the eruption of mass protests erupted as a result of the underground militant movement and this had put India at the weak end. After this situation, India decided to shift its strategy drastically, related to Kashmir. They named this as cross-border terrorism which needed counterinsurgency as a response. However, people involved in this movement did not belong to Pakistan. Their despair related to the political scenario in Kashmir, created by the Indian center, pushed them to take such actions. Believing that bullet was the only solution for Kashmiris, all the Kashmiris (including militants, militant supporters and innocent civilians) were chastised by the Indian central government. The state was suppressed by the center by imposing: curfews and search operations, verbal abuse and humiliation, intimidation, blockage of roads and food supplies, torture, rapes and much more.

All Kashmiris were collectively punished as they were considered the disloyal population of India. This strategy backfired and Kashmir's population started becoming anti-India. India's military response was fierce and successful and it caused the euphoria of Azadi (independence) to dissipate quickly in the 1990s. During 1994 and 1995 many militant groups in Kashmir admitted that they could not defeat the Indian state in the military contest and therefore guns were not the solution. The militant violence from 1988 till 2005 indicates that while being contained, militancy was never eradicated from Kashmir. Another aspect to be considered was that India's military success was never an indicator of providing safe life to the ordinary people in Kashmir.

In 1999, militants from Pakistan invaded the Kargil area of Ladakh. Indian army got to know about the infiltration of militants an intense fight between the Indian army and invading militants continued for more than two months. Indian army managed to reclaim most of the area occupied by the invaders. The hostilities ended when the Prime Minister of Pakistan, Nawaz Sharif, offered his guarantee that infiltrators would evacuate. However, shelling continued across the line of control until 2004 when the cease-fire agreement was reached. After this agreement, the tensions in the region diminished and the relationship between India and Pakistan became more cordial and this led to greater regional cooperation. A limited passenger bus was launched in 2005 between Muzaffarabad and Srinagar. After the deadly earthquake of 2005, Pakistan and India allowed survivors and relief trucks to cross the borders at different points along the line of control.

In 2008, for the first time after the partition in 1947, the cross-border trade link was opened between the two countries through the Kashmir region. This trade tie allowed trucks to carry locally manufactured goods and operate between Pakistan and India.

Along with these pleasant advances, tensions kept erupting in the region. In 2008, violent protests flared up over control of a piece of land used by Hindu pilgrims while visiting the Amarnath shrine located at the east of Srinagar. Again, in 2010, another conflict arose when Indian soldiers killed three Pakistani villagers and claimed that they were militants. The follow-up investigation revealed that the soldiers had lured them to enter the area and then killed them.

In 2014, this unrest in the region got worse when the Hindu nationalist Bhartiya Janata Party (BJP) won elections across India. After winning the election with the outright majority, the party started pushing policies to promote Hindutva (Hinduness). BJP had always supported the accession of Kashmir to India and it became the second-largest party in the Jammu and Kashmir Legislative Assembly. As pro-Indian and Hindutva policies of BJP started to provoke anxieties in the region's population, predominantly Muslims, Kashmir faced enhanced unrest. The growing tensions took the form of riots in July 2016 after the commander of an Islamic militant group was killed by the Indian forces during an operation. The Indian dominion started asserting increased control over the region and classified these riots as a matter of threat to national security followed by the launch of a crackdown on militants.

In late 2018, the Indian central government dissolved the government of Jammu and Kashmir and started ruling the state directly. This happened after BJP left the state's unity coalition and the coalition collapsed. In February 2019, Kashmir experienced the greatest friction in decades. On 14th February 2019, a suicide bomber associated with a militant group killed 40 members of India's Central Reserve Police Force. This was the deadliest attack on Indian forces in three decades. The Indian government claimed that the attack was planned and conducted by Pakistan. However, Pakistan denied this claim.

After this attack, India's BJP led government faced a lot of pressure from its supporters to take strong action. As the tough election cycle was approaching a few days later, India sent fighter jets across Kashmir's line of control for the first time in five decades and later claimed to have conducted an airstrike against the militant groups' largest training camp. This claim was also denied by Pakistan while highlighting that the jets had struck empty fields.

The very next day, Pakistan shot down two Indian jets that entered its flying space and captured a pilot. It was felt that Pakistan did not want to escalate the issue and therefore decided to return the captured Indian pilot to India. As a result of the escalation, Pakistan also implemented a crackdown on militants in the country by closing a large number of religious schools (madrassas), issuing arrests, and aspired to update its existing laws.

BJP won the elections again and expanded its representation in the lower chamber of the parliament as well. The central government strengthened its military presence in Kashmir in August 2019, as BJP kept pushing the forceful actions in the state of Jammu and Kashmir. After strengthening the military control in the region, the Indian government revoked the special status given to Kashmiris under article 370 of the Indian constitution and formalized the direct control of the central government in Kashmir. Exploiting the constitutional provision, Jammu and Kashmir's autonomy was suspended and Indian constitution was applied completely in Kashmir. This revocation was followed by the imposition of curfew and cut down of all communication channels in the state of Jammu and Kashmir.

Recently in 2019, Indian Union Home Minister Amit Shah said that Nehru's decision to internationalize Kashmir's issue and taking it to the United Nations was a blooper, while calling it a "Himalayan Blunder". According to Amit Shah, another mistake from Nehru's end was choosing the wrong article in the UN Charter. Instead of Article 35, the government of India should have chosen Article 51 i.e. illegal occupation of India land by Pakistan. The stance of Indian home minister has clearly indicated that what Kashmiri people want is not relevant, it is that land and its ownership which is relevant. Let's not forget that Kashmir was never a part of India from the very beginning!

Normal life has still NOT been restored in Kashmir and it is under a partial shutdown. The autonomy of the Kashmiri people was taken away with the stroke of a pen. The question arises, *"Can unity be achieved with force?"*

Chapter VII – The War Propaganda and Media

The media of India and Pakistan has been fighting a proxy war for years now. This war has been clouding the unbiased and factual coverage of events happening in the region. Nationalism and jingoism have stayed at the heart of this war. Anchors, journalists, and analysts have remained busy in exposing the hypocrisy and prejudice of the other side. This process has been further abusing the 64-year-old injury.

"When the nation is at war, reporting becomes an extension of that war", Max Hastings, correspondent, Falklands War.

Media of both sides, i.e. India and Pakistan is playing a very negative role and warmongering for their respective governments. When we check the news, we can see that Indian media keeps pointing fingers on Pakistan while Pakistan being in denial mode keeps denying the blames. This is because media has always been used by the governments of Pakistan and India as an outlet to project their official stance on the Kashmir issue.

Warmongering

Pakistani media keeps covering Kashmir issues and positively frames Kashmiri freedom struggles. Indian media usually covers these stories in a negative frame while calling the Kashmiri freedom fighters as militants. Indian media keeps blaming Pakistan's Intelligence for supporting the militancy in Indian administered Kashmir and this stance was supported by Indian government since the Kashmir issue began. For this purpose, they sometimes twist facts and cloud the reality and when people see the falsehood spread against them, the hatred only multiples. Everyone is aware that people in Kashmir have limited access to communication channels and therefore whatever is being portrayed on media is usually one-sided. The Indian government has restricted the access of free media to the people of Indian administered Kashmir. Therefore, the other side of the picture is difficult to see.

Even the Pakistani media does not have access to the on the ground realities as they don't have reporters on ground and their coverage is mostly through secondary sources like Western media, phone calls, social media, etc. This kind of information can either be true or untrue. However, Indian media has reporters in Kashmir which give them credibility to report the realities which are sometimes twisted to project the warmongering agenda. If the media will not act responsibly, the hatred and violence in Kashmir would keep growing and it would become a vicious cycle.

It has been observed on both sides (Pakistan and India) that some senior journalists keep pointing fingers on the other side's government and keep blaming them for the Kashmir issue. We have never seen anyone giving a proposal to resolve the Kashmir conflict peacefully. For political reasons media keeps glorifying war and keeps portraying peaceful resolution as a weakness.

Shouting! ... blaming! ... accusing! ... This is what we see on talk shows these days. The louder your voice, the more are the chances to win an argument on media. At this point, we must remind ourselves that the quality of our argument matters more than our volume. Honestly, this is not about the journalists or mainstream media or political leaders only, this is about us too.

This warmongering media is what we appreciate; this yelling and finger-pointing are what we want to see on our televisions for entertainment purposes. The media has to make money and it will keep showing us what we want to see. After all, it is all about the rating of the program and channel. However, if you look at the demand side, ask yourself, would you be interested in watching a program that blames the other side (either India or Pakistan)? Would you be interested in programs that highlight what wrong the other side has done and portray them as 'bad-cop' just to score points internationally? Or, would you want to watch a program focusing on transforming the Kashmir conflict between India and Pakistan and discussing the peaceful resolution? The answers to these questions would help you to identify that media keeps glorifying war and why it keeps adding to the war propaganda.

In February 2019, during the latest conflict between Pakistan and India, two fighter planes entered Pakistan's airspace and were shot down. The pilot, Wing Commander – Abhinandan Varthaman, was captured by Pakistani authorities. The pilot was returned to India on March 1, 2019.

The Prime Minister of Pakistan, Imran Khan, announced the release of the Indian pilot as a *"peace gesture"*. Many media reports said that Khan was lauded globally for this gesture as a "true statesman". On the other end, Indian media reported that Pakistan had *"cracked under pressure"*. According to some media reports Khan also mentioned that we returned the pilot because we wanted to act responsibly. Sending the pilot back seems to be a peace offering to us but media on both sides covered this matter in a way that projected abhorrence instead of peace. Indian media reported, *"Pakistan did this under international pressure"* and termed this as *"diplomatic victory of New*

Delhi". On the other hand, instead of focusing on peace-building, Pakistani media created hype about the release of the pilot and used this to point fingers towards India by reporting, *"Pakistan shows grit in the face of Indian hostilities"*. This was how a sincere peace gesture was twisted in a hateful, war boosting, propaganda by the media on both sides.

The blame-game mindset is not limited to journalists. These days political leaders of both countries use twitter to blame each other for the unrest in the Kashmir region. Hashtags, full of hatred, keep trending among the two nuclear-armed nations. However, not all political leaders participate in the blame game. Some sensible people still want a peaceful settlement of Kashmir conflict and they keep tweeting to calm the unrest and this is what is expected from sensible and responsible politicians.

Media for Hate or for Education?

Now the question is that just for fame and rating; or re-tweets and appreciation, how can we put the whole region at stake? With each program, with each tweet, with each article, we are pouring hatred in the people of both: India and Pakistan. History has shown us many times that hatred could never resolve anything, but it created division in the region which has led to the downfall.

India and Pakistan are both nuclear-armed countries and the mainstream media of these countries should be cognizant of this fact. Instead of focusing on blame-game and finger-pointing, they should focus more on educating people about the disastrous impacts of nuclear conflict. Media in both countries is free and it has the right to express freely. With this right, comes the greater responsibility of being mature and critical about the claims made by their armies, governments and other non-state actors. Public opinion must be driven by truth and reality and not by jingoism.

From the perspective of ethical journalism, it is recommended that the Kashmir issues be presented with the crucial concerns, informed via facts/data and optimistic presentation. This would allow the national and international peace-building actors to understand the true picture of the scenario and put their efforts towards resolving this conflict peacefully.

Pakistan and India should give access to journalists from neutral press/media including Western media, to gain a neutral or an outsider view on what is happening on the ground. This might help the United Nations and other humanitarian bodies to provide much-needed support to Kashmiri people.

Chapter VIII – Towards Resolution

Kashmir, a rugged land rich in natural resources and nature's beauty, is situated in a very important geo-strategic Asian region. This nature enriched valley has always acted as a bone of contention and has kept the two neighboring South Asian countries, Pakistan and India, on a dangerous course of confrontation since its inception. Both the countries have been embroiled in a territorial battle over Kashmir for more than six decades. Kashmir conflict has acted as a triggering factor and major acrimonious behind the three wars between the two rivals: Pakistan and India. It paved the way to fierceness and brought the two countries to the brink of a nuclear catastrophe. Since 1998, it has been described as a nuclear flashpoint. Moreover, a tremendous drain of resources incurred by two countries on military buildup and arms race has immensely contributed to damaging the economy badly. Hence Kashmir issue appears to be the most thorny, obdurate and intractable dispute between India and Pakistan.

The relationship between Kashmir and India

Presently, India and Pakistan each administer a portion of Kashmir and both claim this Himalayan territory in their entirety and integral territorial region. Kashmiris always insisted that article 370 was a permanent part of the Indian constitution, the hinge upon which the state's relationship with the union was based. After the dissolution of article 370, curfew was imposed to halt retaliation from Kashmiris and still, the life in Jammu and Kashmir has not gone back to normal.

The relationship between Kashmir and India under article 370 is very analogous to a husband-wife relationship. Where the husband has tried everything, which was possible, to retain the relationship and wife wants independence or in other words: divorce. Finally, as the last move, the husband cuts all the phone lines and communication channels and detains the wife inside the house to achieve unity in their relationship; by force. Is that going to work?

Kashmir has a similar story. India has tried everything to keep Kashmir united with India and still Kashmiri's were always keen to achieve independence. As a last try India dissolved article 370, which secured the autonomous status of Jammu and Kashmir, and used military to forcefully engulf Kashmir into Indian dominion. Perhaps this can help India to achieve short term satisfaction, but this strategy can never be successful in the longer run.

Kashmir issue is a stubborn and unresolved lingering issue that has caused distress between the two neighbors i.e. India and Pakistan. This issue has to be resolved in order to ensure regional peace in South-Asia.

A huge chunk of Pakistan's budget is allocated to border security and military acquisition and the same is the case on the other side of the border, in India. Both sides need the money allocated for military spending to deal with other priority issues prevailing in the countries e.g. poverty, hunger, health, education, etc. The military spending on both sides is an indication of an intention for conflict instead of actively looking for strategies to solve this issue. Another important fact to consider in regard to Kashmir is that Kashmiri people do not participate in elections. During the last elections, the turnout was only 2 percent which indicated that 98 percent of people remained passive and did not vote. This is a clear signal that the people in Kashmir want independence and political autonomy. India, at this point, needs to realize that if this dispute lingers on, it can stifle the economic growth of the country. As India is one of the top emerging economic markets in the world.

In 1948, United Nations Security Council Resolution 47 recommended a three-step process for the disputed territory of Kashmir. In the first round, Pakistan was asked to withdraw its nationals from the Kashmir region. The second step was that India was asked to lessen its forces to a minimum for regulating law and order. In the third step India was asked to appoint a plebiscite administrator, nominated by the United Nations Secretary General, who would conduct an impartial plebiscite.

To be fair, Kashmiri people have suffered the most as a result of all the planned propaganda. They need immediate termination of hostilities and conduction of fair plebiscite without intrusion from any of the neighboring countries (Pakistan or India). This plebiscite shall be in accordance with the aspirations and consents of local Kashmiri population. In this case, if mediation from the United Nations is required, the United Nations can get involved to ensure transparency and neutrality.

All the wars between India and Pakistan and decades of conflict have yielded nothing and have rather put the region under constant economic and political instability. Mass rebellions, rallies, and military surveillance create a constant disruption in the normal mode of life in Kashmir. Random arrests, curfews, raids, military checkpoints and arbitrary executions lead to the promotion of extremism, out of despair and oppression, in the region. The military presence and use of force in Kashmir will asphyxiate the economic development in the region. Violence and war can provide short-term victories to either side but both sides lose in the longer run. Don't forget that parents of the suicide bomber in Pulwama stated that their son took the violent route to take revenge from the Indian army after being beaten up by the Indian army a few years ago. This statement makes it clear that violence instigates more violence.

Consider the case of Japan where, before World War-II (WW-II), wars were glorified. During this period of Japanese imperialism, war crimes committed by the Japanese military could be felt in many Asia-Pacific countries. During this time, Japan's education system was also militarized and led to brainwashing children during WW-II. But what happened? The violence and wars led to the nuclear bombing of Hiroshima and Nagasaki, ultimately causing huge social, environmental and economic loss. This moment was recorded in Japanese history as a learnable moment and they changed their constitution and inserted Article-9 which says: *"Aspiring sincerely to an international peace based on justice and order, the Japanese people forever renounce war as a sovereign right of the nation and the threat or use of force as means of settling international disputes.*

In order to accomplish the aim of the preceding paragraph, land, sea, and air forces, as well as other war potential, will never be maintained. The right of belligerency of the state will not be recognized."

Based on Article-9 Japan was demilitarized and they changed their education system which glorified wars. The textbooks of history and geography not only describes the victimized view of Japan highlighting the after-effects of the atomic bombing, but also the real history of Japanese invasion in Korea, China, and other Asia-Pacific countries. They did this to make sure that this kind of man-made, war-induced, disaster should never happen again. With this backdrop, in order to improve or progress and build peace, it is important to accept our own mistakes in the history first and then formulate policies in different sectors based on lessons from past mistakes. Japan takes peace-building this seriously because they have suffered through a nuclear war. Pakistan and India being nuclear powers need to realize that if the war breaks out, both sides will suffer badly. We don't need to go through a nuclear conflict to see the importance of peace! Why do we have to wage war to see the significance of peace? We can clearly see from the history of conflict-stricken regions of the world, none of them support wars now.

Kashmir resolution is important because it is the birthright of every Kashmiri to be free and decide their destiny. Therefore, it is our responsibility to ensure that they get this liberty and they do not face any limitation in this regard. Conflicts have never solved anything but induced other challenges. Therefore, peaceful settlement of Kashmir issue with the help of negotiations, dialogues, and bilateral mutual cooperation is important to promote economic stability in the region and development in both Pakistan and India. Peaceful resolution of Kashmir dispute will create an environment of mutual respect, peace, and harmony in South-Asia.

Three-tiered approach

Keeping that in mind, at the moment, the Pak-India relationship is in a terribly damaged condition. Therefore, both sides need to understand that it will not be easy to resolve the Kashmir issue; but it is very crucial resolving this issue if they want peace in the region and development in the respective countries. In this section of the book, we want to propose a three-tiered approach to deal with Kashmir issue peacefully. This approach includes: (i) Building trust to set the ground for peace talks and negotiations; (ii) Free and fair plebiscite; (iii) The last resort – International Court of Justice.

Tier-1: Building Trust

Every relationship starts with trust and if we examine the bilateral relationship between Pakistan and India, it is only about conflict. Trust cannot be seen anywhere near Pak-India bilateral relationship. As a first step, we want to propose that empathy and creativity should be used to rewrite and rewire the relationship between Pakistan and India. Both states are facing similar issues like water shortage, energy insecurity, food shortage, etc. The change in focus might normalize the relationship through sharing solutions for common problems. This will help both sides to build trust on each other and set the ground for having peace talks and negotiations.

In the process of building trust, we want to highlight the importance of peace education. It is important to teach young children of both countries the true history, NOT the CONSPIRED one, including what had gone wrong in the past. This will make sure that the region achieves peace and prosperity. If we will keep on teaching our kids and young generation the conspired history with a one-sided perspective, we will never be able to identify what had gone wrong and we can never progress. Children should be taught about the horrors of wars by discussing the war case-studies, and we have enough of them globally. We don't need to be a case ourselves in order to teach our next generations about the horrors of wars and conflicts. Teaching true history on both sides will automatically acknowledge that each side has accepted their fault and aim to take the responsibility of correcting that. This will definitely strengthen the foundation of trust-building.

We remember having a conversation with one of our friends managing an exchange program between India and Pakistan. This exchange program was planned for junior-high-school (middle-school) students. She told us that during the program students in Pakistan wrote letters to their counterparts in India and Indian students then replied to their letters and this series of letter exchange continued for four rounds, followed by a physical exchange between students.

She highlighted that: "The initial exchange was very blunt as Pakistani students were curious about Indian students. Some of them clearly asked, *Do you like Pakistan?*" and "*... told me that India is our enemy*". These statements were not coming from the students but either from their family members, media or conspired history books. This curiosity was not one-sided; students from India also had similar questions which meant that they were in a similar situation. By the time they finished the last round of letter exchange, their point of view about their counterparts on both sides changed. This letter exchange had set a very friendly tone and we had an amicable exchange with Indian school".

Exchange programs, not only at the school-level but also at the university-level, can help in building collaboration and clearing misunderstandings. Therefore, it is suggested to encourage student-exchange programs between India and Pakistan in order to build trust in each other.

"Building trust" is easy to write but very difficult to practice. If both states will be willing to build a bilateral relationship based on trust and transform the conflict-based relationship into an amicable one, they will need to act in a certain way to make sure that the trust does not get shattered on either side.

Pakistan has always denied taking the responsibility of training militants, but Pakistan is well aware that militants are getting support from its soil. This can be in the form of in-formal facilities set up by individuals in the autonomous region of Kashmir administered by Pakistan or in other regions of Pakistan. Pakistan needs to put more efforts to severely scrutinize the informal organizations operating, in the name of religion, in Pakistan or Kashmir region administered by Pakistan. It is very evident that during the last few years, Pakistan has taken a lot of steps to ensure that terrorists should not operate from its soil. However, if any kind of support is being given to the militants who are fighting the Indian security forces in Jammu and Kashmir, formally or informally, that shall be congested instantly. On the other hand, Research and Analysis Wing (RAW) as a part of the intelligence services of India has been historically active in creating disruptions and violations in Pakistan. If RAW is creating troubles in Pakistan regarding Kashmir issue in order to blame Pakistan in front of an international audience, it should be put to an end. Putting such activities to a complete stop, on both sides, is crucial as they are against the international laws and vital for starting peace talks.

When people are deprived of their basic rights, they are vulnerable and that is the time when external political forces come in to play. These people, out of their vulnerability, get exploited and controlled by external political forces. These forces brainwash them, nurture hatred and use these people for their benefit. This is exactly what happened in Kashmir. Both sides need to understand this.

Tier 2: Plebiscite

As a second tier, we can only see plebiscite as a legitimized and authentic way to achieve regional harmony along with political and economic stability. A fair plebiscite would allow free will and rule of the majority to prevail in Kashmir. This might or might not be aligned with what India and Pakistan want. Both Pakistan and India should respect the self-determination of the Kashmiri people and embrace their sovereignty. This plebiscite will truly determine if Kashmiris: (a) Want to stay within Indian dominion; (b) Want to stay within Pakistani dominion; (c) Want to stay independent.

The amicable settlement of the Kashmir dispute will enhance the trade ties and social contracts, allowing both countries to flourish financially in the world's economic market. This dialogue is central for the development and growth of both countries and both Pakistan and India need to understand that peace talks will be a win-win for both parties. International bodies like the United Nations and international think tanks can help in facilitating and mediating peace negotiations between India and Pakistan. Bringing in think tanks from both sides will allow evidence-based, informed decision making and refraining from the blame game. Both sides have proven their respective points and this is the time to end this dispute and reflect on the fact that war and conflicts are not the solutions.

Tier 3: The Last Resort
Lastly, if both sides fail to understand each other perspectives and consensus cannot be reached, then as a last resort, Kashmir issue can be forwarded to the International Court of Justice without violating the bilateral agreement. The decision made by the International Court shall be, peacefully, respected by both countries. We also want to highlight that the third tier to explore the International Court of Justice can be considered as a backup plan. This backup plan will not be required if the first two steps are properly planned and implemented.

Now, Kashmir is not about how much land each country gets but it is a much bigger issue. It is about the people of Kashmir who have been suffering for decades; it is about peaceful sub-continent; and finally, it is about the economic and political stability of the region.

Chapter IX – Let's Reflect

We are well aware of the Corona Virus (COVID 19) outbreak, globally. Most of us are, currently, restricted to our houses. Now we know how it feels on being forcefully locked down; now we know how it feels when we cannot go out because of the fear of dying; now we know how it feels when our children cannot go to school. This is how Kashmiris have been living for so long!

WE NEED TO FOCUS ON THE BIGGER PICTURE!

The current COVID-19 crisis has a lot of similarities with the Kashmir crisis and that is what we will discuss in this chapter. The pandemic has allowed us to see the vulnerability and resilience of Kashmiris who have been living in the condition of crisis for so long.

COVID-19

The COVID-19 issue forced us to stay indoors, in the condition of lock down in many regions of the world, and we all know that lock-down is repressive. We don't know how long it will take to get rid of the Corona virus crisis, we are so vulnerable in the face of this catastrophe but at the same time we still have hope that one day we will be back to our normal routines. Probably, when the scientists will invent vaccine for this virus. This hope allows us to keep standing in the face of adversity and it will make us resilient. Similarly, Kashmiris have been in this state of vulnerability for so long and they have hopes, that they will have freedom. This hope forces them to raise their voices and act in rebellious ways. The bloodbath will keep happening till

Kashmiri's have hope of freedom in their hearts and minds... We definitely don't want to kill this hope!! Think!

During COVID-19 crisis most people are confined to their houses and during this time internet, technology and communication are crucial to maintain our sanity. During the lock down period, when you cannot see your loved ones, it is important to connect with them virtually to maintain the connectivity and support system. Imagine yourself without communication channels, internet connection or other mass media access, during this isolation period. How will you feel? Kashmiri's are facing communication and internet restrictions for so long; can you imagine now who does their life look like? Many Kashmir's have not met and spoken to their closest and even blood relatives for so long. Parents have not seen their children, and they can't speak to their children.... Has COVID-19 issue made it easy for us to empathize with the situation of Kashmiris?

Unfortunately, we have become so self-absorbed!!! I have a question that why haven't we heard about any war mongering news or any war related news since COVID-19 outbreak? Is that because states are so busy in dealing with their own people and internal issues that they have no time to focus on war? Why can't we do this forever? Without any virus outbreak? India and Pakistan are developing countries, there is a lot to fix in both countries and solving Kashmir issue, peacefully, will allow them to focus on their internal challenges (i.e. poverty, access to quality education, health care etc.) and collaborate with each other instead of focusing on conflicts and war.

Both Pakistan and India invest a lot in military or defense (in other words war), instead of investing on education or healthcare. This became very evident with the Corona virus outbreak. We definitely need more investment and focus on education and healthcare instead of wars and defense. Military equipment did not help us bounce back from the invisible COVID-19 crisis.

Corona virus is a pandemic and so are wars! Even if the war is happening in one area, the whole region, and even world, deals with the consequences of that. This is a call for reflecting and focusing on bigger picture...

Solve the Kashmir conflict peacefully with negotiation because building peace is far easier than bearing the consequences and horrors of conflict!

Acknowledgement

We want to thank Ms. Tooba Irfan Haider for reading the first draft of the book and suggesting some language edits.

References

[1] Ahmad, I. (2005). Competing Religious Nationalism and the Partition of British India. *Pakistan Journal Of History & Culture, 26*(2), 1-11.

[2] Ahmed, I. (2002). The 1947 partition of India: A paradigm for pathological politics in India and Pakistan. *Asian ethnicity, 3*(1), 9-28.

[3] Ali, C. R. (1933). Now or never: Are we to live or perish for ever?. *Cambridge: The Pakistan National Movement.*

[4] Allana, G. (1969). Pakistan Movement Historical Documents (Karachi: Department of International Relations, University of Karachi, pp. 407-411.

[5] Aslam, R. (2014). *The role of media in conflict: Integrating peace journalism in the journalism curriculum* (Doctoral dissertation, Auckland University of Technology).

[6] Avari, B. (2016). *India: The ancient past: A history of the Indian subcontinent from C. 7000 BCE to CE 1200.* Routledge.

[7] Behera, N. C. (2007). *Demystifying Kashmir.* Brookings Institution Press.

[8] Bose, S. (2009). *Kashmir: Roots of conflict, paths to peace.* Harvard University Press.

[9] David Gilmartin (2015). The Historiography of India's Partition: Between Civilization and Modernity. The Journal of Asian Studies, 74, pp 23-41 doi:10.1017/S0021911814001685

[10] Farrell, B. (2002). The Role of International Law in the Kashmir Conflict. *Penn St. Int'l L. Rev., 21*, 293.

[11] Ganguly, S. (1989). Avoiding war in Kashmir. *Foreign Aff., 69*, 57.

[12] Graff, D. F. (1952). The Kashmir question in the Security Council 1958-1952.

[13] Khan, Y. (2017). *The great partition: The making of India and Pakistan.* Yale University Press.

[14] Korbel, J. (1953). Danger in Kashmir. *Foreign Aff., 32*, 482.

[15] Marshall, P. J. (1975). British Expansion in India in the Eighteenth Century: A Historical Revision. *History*, *60*(198), 28-43.

[16] Marshall, P. J. (2006). *Bengal: The British Bridgehead: Eastern India 1740-1828* (Vol. 2). Cambridge University Press.

[17] Menon, R., & Bhasin, K. (1998). *Borders & boundaries: women in India's partition*. Rutgers University Press.

[18] Mohan, A. (1992). The historical roots of the Kashmir conflict. *Studies in Conflict & Terrorism*, *15*(4), 283-308.

[19] Pillalamarri, A. (2019). The Origins of Hindu-Muslim Conflict in South Asia. What are the historical origins of animosities between South Asia's two largest religions? Available at: https://thediplomat.com/2019/03/the-origins-of-hindu-muslim-conflict-in-south-asia/, Accessed December 12, 2019.

[20] Ray, Rajat Kanta. "Book Reviews: SUMIT SARKAR, Writing Social History, Oxford University Press, Delhi, 1997, pp. 390, Rs 495." *The Indian Economic & Social History Review* 35, no. 2 (1998): 222-224.

[21] Reayat, N., Veesrio, M. A., & Baloch, S. (2015). QUAID-E-AZAM MOHAMMAD ALI JINNAH'S ROLE IN HINDU-MUSLIM UNITY: A CASE OF UNITY OF TWO CLASSES. *Grassroots, 49*(2).

[22] Schofield, V. (2010). *Kashmir in conflict: India, Pakistan and the unending war*. Bloomsbury Publishing.

[23] Sehgal, R. (2011). Kashmir conflict: Solutions and demand for self-determination. *International Journal of Humanities and Social Science, 1*(6).

[24] Sidhu, W. P. S., Asif, B., & Samii, C. (Eds.). (2006). *Kashmir: New voices, new approaches*. Lynne Rienner Publishers.

[25] Talbot, I., & Singh, G. (2009). *The partition of India* (p. 30). Cambridge: Cambridge University Press.

[26] Tavares, R. (2008). Resolving the Kashmir conflict: Pakistan, India, Kashmiris and religious militants. *Asian Journal of Political Science, 16*(3), 276-302.

[27] Thapar, Valmik. *Land of the Tiger: A Natural History of the Indian subcontinent*. Univ of California Press, 1997.

[28] Viswam, D. (2010). *Role of media in Kashmir crisis*. Gyan Publishing House.

[29] Wani, H. A., & Suwirta, A. (2014). United Nations Involvement in Kashmir Conflict. SUSURGALUR, 2(1)

[30] Zaheer, L. (2016). War or Peace Journalism: Comparative analysis of Pakistan's English and Urdu media coverage of Kashmir conflict. *South Asian Studies*, *31*(2), 713-722.

Diplomatic Council

The present work was published by the Diplomatic Council publishing house.

The Diplomatic Council (DC) combines a global think tank, a business network and a charity foundation in a unique organization with consultant status at the United Nations.
Our members are firmly convinced that economic diplomacy is a fundamental foundation for international understanding and peaceful dealings between nations.

Further information: www.diplomatic-council.org